Contents

1   **INTRODUCTION**

ACT I—The "Before" Phase

27   Chapter 1—Selecting Your Target Market
39   Chapter 2—Crafting Your Message
73   Chapter 3—Reaching Prospects With Advertising Media

ACT II—The "During" Phase

95   Chapter 4—Capturing Leads
103   Chapter 5—Nurturing Leads
123   Chapter 6—Sales Conversion

ACT III—The "After" Phase

147   Chapter 7—Delivering A World Class Experience
171   Chapter 8—Increasing Customer Lifetime Value
193   Chapter 9—Orchestrating And Stimulating Referrals

205   **CONCLUSION**

215   About The Author

Acknowledgements

*"If I have seen further than others, it is by standing upon
the shoulders of giants."*

—Isaac Newton

I wish I could tell you all the ideas in this book were my inventions and that I'm some kind of marketing and business genius. The truth though is I'm a collector of elegant ideas. I rarely invent anything and when I do, it's rarely worth writing about.

An early business mentor of mine, Mal Emery would often say, "I've never had an original idea in my life—it's just too bloody dangerous." Yet he was and continues to be an extremely successful businessman and marketer. The secret of his success and subsequently mine, was to just model things that were known to reliably work rather than trying to reinvent the wheel.

Reinventing the wheel requires you to be a genius and even then, it carries with it a high probability of failure. I'm no genius and I hate failing, so I prefer to just closely copy the things that made others successful—at least until I've got a very good handle on the basics. This tilts the odds in my favor and gives me a high probability of success.

While I did create the system that has become The 1-Page Marketing Plan, many of the direct response marketing concepts that make it work are the invention and ideas of other great business leaders and marketers.

Perhaps I flatter myself but the aphorism, *"Good artists copy; great artists steal."* repeated by Steve Jobs and attributed to Pablo Picasso is certainly a philosophy I've held in mind when collecting these elegant ideas over the years and writing this book. Regardless of whether you consider me a "great artist" or a thief, I want you to benefit from the treasure trove of the proven business-building ideas that follow.

Certainly there's a place for creativity and invention but in my opinion, this should come after you've first mastered the basics. This book

v

contains many of those basics. Some come from my own experiences but most from people who've been "giants" in my business life and on whose shoulders I've stood. In no particular order I'd like to acknowledge:

Mal Emery

Dean Jackson

Joe Polish

Pete Godfrey

Dan Kennedy

James Schramko

Jim Rohn

Frank Kern

Seth Godin

Some have been personal mentors to me, while others have been mentors to me through publications and other works they've produced. I try and credit them in footnotes throughout this book when, as far as I know, an idea I'm presenting has originated from them. However, I'm certain that I've left other people out or not acknowledged enough of the ideas of the people above. When you collect ideas over a period of many years it can sometimes become a blur when trying to recall where one originated. For that I apologize in advance.

The 1-Page Marketing Plan is to be an implementation break-through, rather than a new marketing innovation or concept. It's by far the easiest way for a small business to go from knowing nothing about marketing to creating and implementing a sophisticated direct response marketing plan in their business. The plan is literally reduced to a single page.

Please enjoy the ideas in this book and more importantly **implement** them in your business. Remember knowing and not doing is the same as not knowing.

> <u>Important</u>: Download your copy of the companion resources for this book at 1pmp.com Resources include templates and samples of the 1-Page Marketing Plan as well as links, videos and articles referenced throughout this book.

Introduction

What's This All About?

If I had to summarize the essence of this book in one sentence it would be, "**the fastest path to the money.**" I've purposely put this as early as humanly possible in the book because I don't want to waste your time.

I know for a certainty that this opening sentence will be off-putting to a large number of people and frankly I'd much prefer they read someone else's business book full of ear-tickling clichés like "follow your passion," "work hard," "hire the right people," blah blah blah.

If that's what you're after, then search Amazon. There'll be a gazillion business books there for you on all these airy fairy concepts and much more, mostly written by professional authors and researchers who've never actually built a high growth business.

This book is blatantly and unashamedly about growing your business fast and reaping the rewards of that kind of success.

Running Out Of Oxygen Really Sucks

As Zig Ziglar famously said, "Money isn't everything…but it ranks right up there with oxygen."

Yup, nothing—NOTHING—kills a business faster than a lack "oxygen" (aka money).

Why am I so unashamedly focused on the money getting? There are a few good reasons.

Firstly, there's almost no business problem that can't be solved with more money. Which is handy because almost every business I know of is full of problems. Money helps you solve the vast majority of things that make business a pain in the backside.

Secondly, when you've taken care of yourself, you have a chance to help others.

If you didn't go into business to make money then you're either lying or you have a hobby, not a business. And yes I know all about delivering value, changing the world, etc. but how much of that are you going to do if you're broke? How many people can you help?

When you board an airplane and they're going through all the safety procedures, the airline attendant will inevitably get to a point that goes something like this:

*"Should the cabin experience sudden pressure loss, oxygen masks will drop down from above your seat. Place the mask over your mouth and nose and pull the strap to tighten. If you are traveling with children or someone who requires assistance, **make sure that your own mask is on first before helping others**."*

Why fit your own mask before helping others? Because if you're slumped over your seat suffering from a lack of oxygen;

a. you can't help anyone else, and even worse;
b. we now have to deploy scarce resources to come and help you, otherwise you'll soon be dead.

Knowing What To Do

In his book titled, *The Book of Survival*, Anthony Greenback wrote;

"To live through an impossible situation, you don't need to have the reflexes of a Grand Prix driver, the muscles of a Hercules, the mind of an Einstein. You simply need to know what to do."

The statistics vary on exactly what percentage of businesses fail within the first five years. Some estimates put it as high as 90%. However, I've never seen this statistic being quoted at anything less than

50%. That means that if we're being super-optimistic you have a 50/50 chance of still having your doors open after five years.

However, here's where it really gets worse. The statistics only take into account businesses that completely cease trading. They don't take into account the businesses that plateau at a low level and slowly kill or make the lives of their owners miserable.

Have you ever wondered why most small businesses plateau at a mediocre level?

At one end of the spectrum there's Pete the plumber who works sixteen-hour days, weekends and never takes holidays while barely making enough to keep his head above water. On the other end of the spectrum there's Joe who runs a plumbing company with twenty plumbers working for him. It seems like his primary business activity is counting the huge sums of money that keep rolling in.

It's very common for small businesses to never grow past the point at which they generate just enough profit for the owner(s) to make a modest living. It seems that no matter how hard the owner(s) try, their efforts to get to the next level just lead to frustration. At this point one of two things happens. Either they get disillusioned or they just accept their fate—that their business is nothing more than a low-paid, self-created job.

In fact the reality is that many business owners would probably be better off just finding a job in their industry. They would likely work fewer hours, have less stress, enjoy more benefits and more holiday time than in the prison they have created for themselves. On the flip side, there are a few business owners that just seem to have it all. They work reasonable hours, have a fantastic cash flow from their enterprise and enjoy continuous growth.

Many business owners who are struggling blame their industry. While it's true some industries are in decline—examples such as book stores or video rental stores immediately come to mind. If you are in one of these dead or dying industries it may be time to cut your losses and move on, rather than torture yourself to death financially. This may be particularly difficult if you have been in the industry for a long time.

However, for the most part, when people blame their industry they are just playing the blame game. Some of the most common industry complaints I hear are:

- It's too competitive
- The margins are too low
- Online discounters are taking customers away
- Advertising no longer works

However, it's rarely the industry that is truly to blame, after all there are others in that same industry that are doing very well. So the obvious question is what are they doing differently?

Many small business owners fall into the trap described in Michael Gerber's classic book, *The E-Myth*. That is they are a technician, e.g. plumber, hairdresser, dentist etc., and they are good at what they do. They have what Gerber describes as an "entrepreneurial seizure" and they start to think to themselves, "Why should I work for this idiot boss of mine? I'm good at what I do—I'll start my own business."

This is one of THE major mistakes made by most small business owners. They go from working for an idiot boss to **becoming** an idiot boss! Here is the key point—just because you're good at the technical thing you do doesn't mean that you are good at the **business** of what you do.

So going back to our example, a good plumber is not necessarily the best person to run a plumbing business. This is a vitally important distinction to note and is a key reason that most small businesses fail. The owner of the business may have excellent technical skills but it's his lack of business skills that causes his business to fail.

This is not meant to discourage people from starting their own businesses. However, you must resolve to become good at the business of what you do—not just the technical thing you do. A business can be an amazing vehicle for achieving financial freedom and personal fulfillment—but only for those who understand and master this vital distinction and figure out what they need to do to run a successful business.

If you're good at the technical thing of what you do but feel like you could benefit from some help on the business side, then you're in

4

the right place at the right time. The whole point of this book is to take you from confusion to clarity—so you know exactly what to do to have business success.

Professionals Have Plans

As a kid my favorite TV show was *The A-Team*. In case you've never watched it, I'll give you the executive summary of 99% of the episodes:

1. Bad guys harass and threaten an innocent person or group
2. The innocent person or group begs and pleads with the A-Team to help them
3. The A-Team (a motley bunch of ex-soldiers) humiliate and drive away the bad guys

Episodes would invariably end with Hannibal (the brains of the A-Team) chomping down on his cigar and triumphantly mumbling, "I love it when a plan comes together."

Look at any profession where the stakes are high and you'll see a well-thought-out plan being followed. **Professionals never just wing it.**

Doctors follow a treatment plan.

Airline pilots follow a flight plan.

Soldiers follow a military operation plan.

How would you feel about engaging the services of any of the above professions where the practitioner says to you "screw the plan, I'll just wing it." Yet this is exactly what most business owners do.

Invariably, when someone makes a mess of something it often becomes clear in the aftermath that they didn't have a plan. Don't let that be you and your business. While no one can guarantee your success, having a plan dramatically increases your probability of success.

Just like you wouldn't want to be on a plane where the pilot hadn't bothered with a flight plan, you don't want you and your family relying on a business where you hadn't bothered with a business plan. Often the stakes are almost as high. Marriages, partnerships, jobs and more are often the casualties of failed businesses.

It's more than just your ego on the line so it's time to "go pro" and create a plan.

The Wrong Kind Of Plan

Early into my first business I was smart enough to identify that a business plan was going to be important to my success. Unfortunately that's where my smarts ended.

With the help of a business consultant (who'd never actually run a successful business of his own), I ended up many thousands of dollars poorer but had a document that most business owners never bother with—a **business plan**.

My business plan was many hundreds of pages long. It had graphs, charts, projections and much, much more. It was an awesome looking document but essentially was a bunch of nonsense.

After it was written, I shoved it in the top drawer of my desk and never saw it again until the day we were moving offices and I had to clean out my desk.

I dusted it off, flicked through it and tossed it in the trash, angry at myself about the money I'd wasted on that phony baloney consultant.

However, later when I thought about it more carefully, I realized while the document itself was a bunch of nonsense, the process I went through with the consultant was valuable in clarifying some of the key elements in my business, particularly one key section of it called "the marketing plan."

In fact, a lot of what we did to create the marketing plan shaped the business and created much of our future success.

More on this in a moment but for now let me introduce a man and his concept that's going to be the key to your business success.

My Friend Vilfredo Pareto and the 80/20 Rule

I never had the privilege of meeting Vilfredo Pareto, mostly because he died over half a century before I was born, but I'm sure we would have been best buds.

Pareto was an Italian economist who noticed that 80% of the land in Italy was owned by 20% of the population. Hence the Pareto Principle, commonly known as the 80/20 rule, was born.

It turns out the 80/20 rule holds true for more than just land owner-ship in Italy. It holds true for almost anything you care to think of. Some examples:

80% of a company's profits come from 20% of its customers
80% of road traffic accidents are caused by 20% of drivers
80% of software usage is by 20% of users
80% of a company's complaints come from 20% of its customers
80% of wealth is owned by 20% of people
Woody Allen even noted that 80% of success is showing up.

In other words **the Pareto Principle predicts that 80% of effects come from 20% of causes**.

Maybe it's just my laziness talking, but this gets me seriously excited.

It's often said that necessity is the mother of invention but I'd argue that laziness is and my friend Vilfredo is my mentor in that pursuit.

So essentially you can cut out 80% of the stuff you're doing, sit on the couch eating nachos instead and you'll still get most of the result you're getting.

If you don't want to sit on the couch chowing down on nachos 80% of the time, then doing more of the 20% stuff is your fast track to success. And in this context success = more money with less work.

The 64/4 Rule

If you think the 80/20 is exciting, the 64/4 rule[1] will blow your mind. You see we can apply the 80/20 rule to the rule itself. So we take 80% of 80 and 20% of 20 and end up with the 64/4 rule.

So **64% of effects come from 4% of causes**.

Put another way—the majority of your success comes from the top 4% of your actions. Or put yet another way **96% of the stuff you do is waste of time** (comparatively).

The most surprising thing is that the 80/20 rule and 64/4 rule still hold up in a remarkably accurate way. If you look at wealth distribution statistics from the last century you'll notice that the top 4% own about 64% of wealth and the top 20% own about 80% of the wealth. This is despite this being the "information age." You'd imagine that a hundred years ago only the wealthy had good access to information, hence it's understandable why they held 80% of the wealth. Yet this wealth distribution statistic still holds up today, an age where information has been democratized and where even the poorest people have pretty much the same access to information as the wealthiest people.

This proves that lack of information isn't the issue holding back the bottom 80% of business owners—it's human behavior and mindset. That certainly hasn't changed in the last 100 years.

---

[1] I first heard of the 64/4 rule from James Schramko at his SuperFastBusiness Live event.

The Best Kept Secret Of The Rich

In my observation of and work with numerous business owners around the world there's one thing which differentiates the wildly successful and wealthy ones from the struggling and broke.

Struggling business owners will spend time to save money, whereas successful business owners will spend money to save time. Why is that an important distinction? Because you can always get more money, but you can never get more time. So you need to ensure the stuff you spend your time on makes the biggest impact.

This is called leverage and **leverage is the best kept secret of the rich**.

These big impacting, leveraged activities are the things that make up the key 20% of the 80/20 rule and the 4% of the 64/4 rule.

If you want more success you need to start paying attention to and expand the things that give you the most leverage.

There are various areas of your business where you could start looking for leverage points. You may look at getting 50% better at your negotiation skills. This in turn may help you re-negotiate with key suppliers and get an incremental improvement in your buy price. While this is great, at the end of the day after all that time and effort you've still just improved your bottom line incrementally. This is not what I'd call massive leverage. We want exponential improvement, not incremental.

By far the biggest leverage point in any business is marketing. If you get 10% better at marketing, this can have an exponential or multiplying effect on the bottom line.

Willie Sutton was a prolific American bank robber. During his forty-year criminal career he stole millions of dollars, and eventually spent more than half of his adult life in prison and also managed to escape three times. Sutton was asked by reporter Mitch Ohnstad why he robbed banks. According to Ohnstad, he replied, "Because that's where the money is." When it comes to business the reason we want to focus so heavily on marketing is the same—because **that's where the money is**.

Applying The 80/20 and 64/4 Rules: Your Marketing Plan

Back to my earlier story about the wrong type of business plan. While my business plan document ended up being a useless mess of management speak and nonsense, the part of the business planning process that proved hugely valuable to me was creating the marketing plan.

The marketing plan ended up being the 20% part of the business planning process that produced 80% of the result.

This has been the case in every business I created and ran since then.

With this in mind when I started coaching small business owners, a large part of my focus was getting them to create a marketing plan.

Guess what? Very few of them ever carried through with it. Why? Because creating a marketing plan was a complex, laborious process which most small business owners simply won't do.

So again laziness becomes the mother of invention. I needed a way to take the core essence of the marketing planning process and make it simple, practical and useful to small business owners. The 1-Page Marketing Plan is born.

The 1-Page Marketing Plan is the 4% of effort that generates 64% (or more) of the result in your business. It's the 64/4 rule applied to business planning. Using this process we can boil down hundreds of pages and thousands of hours of traditional business planning in a single page which can take as little as thirty minutes to think about and fill in.

Even more exciting is that it becomes a living document in your business. One that you can stick on the wall of your office and refer to and refine over time. Most of all it's practical. There's no management speak or jargon to understand. You don't need an MBA to create it or understand it.

The 1-Page Marketing Plan has been a marketing implementation breakthrough. I've seen compliance rates among coaching clients significantly improve. Small business owners who would have never had the time, money or knowhow to create a traditional marketing plan now have one. As a result, they've reaped the massive benefits that come from having clarity around their marketing.

I'll introduce the 1-Page Marketing Plan shortly but first I think it would be valuable to start at the beginning and not assume anything. Marketing itself is a vague term which is poorly understood even by so-called professionals and experts in the industry.

So let's quickly get a quick and simple understanding of what marketing actually is.

What Is Marketing?

Some people think marketing is advertising or branding or some other vague concept. While all these are associated with marketing, they are not one and the same.

Here's the simplest, most jargon-free, definition of marketing you're ever likely to come across:

If the circus is coming to town and you paint a sign saying "Circus Coming to the Showground Saturday," that's **advertising**.

If you put the sign on the back of an elephant and walk it into town, that's **promotion**.

If the elephant walks through the mayor's flower bed and the local newspaper writes a story about it, that's **publicity**.

And if you get the mayor to laugh about it, that's **public relations**.

If the town's citizens go to the circus, you show them the many entertainment booths, explain how much fun they'll have spending money at the booths, answer their questions and ultimately, they spend a lot at the circus, that's **sales**.

And if you planned the whole thing, **that's marketing**.

Yup it's as simple as that—marketing is the **strategy** you use for getting your ideal target market to know you, like and trust you enough to become a customer. All the stuff you usually associate with marketing are **tactics**. We'll talk more about strategy vs. tactics in a moment.

However, before we do that you need to understand a fundamental shift has occurred in the last decade and things will never be the same.

The Answers Have Changed

Albert Einstein was once giving an exam paper to his graduating class. It turned out that it was the exact same exam paper he had given them the previous year. His teaching assistant, alarmed at what he saw and thinking it to be the result of the professor's absent-mindedness, alerted Einstein.

"Excuse me, sir," said the shy assistant, not quite sure how to tell the great man about his blunder.

"Yes?" said Einstein.

"Um, eh, it's about the test you just handed out."

Einstein waited patiently.

"I'm not sure if you realize it, but this is the same test you gave out last year. In fact, it's identical."

Einstein paused to think for a moment, then said,

"Yes, it is the same test but the answers have changed."

Just as the answers in physics change as new discoveries are made, so too do the answers in business and in marketing.

Once upon a time you placed an ad in the Yellow Pages, paid them a truck load of money and your marketing for the year was done. Now you have Google, social media, blogs, websites and myriad of other things to think about.

The Internet has literally opened up a world of competitors. Whereas previously your competitors may have been across the road, now they can be on the other side of the globe.

As a result of this many who are trying to market their business become paralyzed by the "bright shiny object syndrome." This is where they get caught up in whatever the currently "hot" marketing **tactics** are like SEO, video, podcasting, pay-per-click advertising, etc.

They get caught up with tools and tactics and never figure out the big picture of what they're trying to actually do and why.

Let me show you why this will lead to a world of pain.

Strategy vs. Tactics

Understanding the difference between strategy and tactics is absolutely key to marketing success.

Strategy is the big-picture planning you do prior to the tactics. Imagine you've bought an empty block of land and want to build a house. Would you just order a pile of bricks and then just start laying them? Of course not. You'd end up with a big old mess that likely wasn't safe.

So what do you do instead? You hire a builder and an architect first and they plan everything out from the major stuff like getting building permits, down to what kind of tap fittings you'd like. All of this is planned prior to a single shovel of dirt being moved. **That's strategy**.

Then once you have your strategy, you know how many bricks you need, where the foundation goes and what kind of roof you're going to have. Now you can hire a brick layer, carpenter, plumber, electrician, etc. **That's tactics**.

You can't do anything worthwhile successfully without both strategy and tactics.

Strategy without tactics leads to paralysis by analysis. No matter how good the builder and the architect are, the house isn't going to get built until someone starts laying bricks. At some stage they're going to need to say, "OK the blueprint is now good, we've got all the necessary approvals to build so let's get started."

Tactics without strategy lead to "bright shiny object syndrome." Imagine you started building a wall without any plans and then later found out that it was in the wrong place, so you start pouring the foundation and then you find out it's not right for this type of house, so you start excavating the area where you want the pool but that isn't right either. This clearly isn't going to work. Yet this is exactly how many business owners do marketing. They string together a bunch of random tactics in the hope that what they're doing will lead to a customer. They whack up a website without much thought and it ends up being an online version of their brochure or they start promoting on social media because they heard that's the latest thing and so on.

You need both strategy and tactics to be successful but strategy must come first and it dictates the tactics you use. This is where your marketing plan comes in. Think of your marketing plan as the architect's blueprint for getting and retaining customers.

I Have Great Product/Service, Do I Really Need Marketing?

Many business owners fool themselves into thinking that if their product is excellent, the market will buy. While *"if you build it, they will come"* makes a great movie plot, it's a terrible business strategy. It's a strategy that's expensive and comes with a high rate of failure. History is littered with technically superior products that commercially failed. A few examples include Betamax, The Newton and LaserDisc to name just a few.

Good, even great, products are simply not enough. Marketing must be one of your major activities if you're to have business success.

Ask yourself, when does a prospect find out how good your product or service is? The answer of course is—when they buy. If they don't buy, they'll never know how good your products or services are. As Thomas Watson from IBM famously said:

"Nothing happens until a sale is made."

Therefore we need to clearly understand an important concept: **a good product or service is a customer retention tool**. If we give our customers a great product or service experience they'll buy more from us, they'll refer other people to us and build up the brand through positive word of mouth. However, before customer **retention**, we need to think about customer **acquisition** (AKA marketing). The most successful entrepreneurs always start with marketing.

How To Kill Your Business

I'm about to reveal to you one of the easiest and most common ways to kill your business—in the earnest hope that you won't do it. It's absolutely the biggest mistake made by small business owners when it comes to marketing.

It's a widespread problem, and it's at the heart of why <u>most small business marketing fails</u>.

If you're a small business owner, you've no doubt given some thought to marketing and advertising. What approach are you going to take? What are you going to say in your advertising?

The most common way most small business owners decide on this is by looking at large, successful competitors in their industry and mimicking what they're doing. This seems logical—do what other successful businesses are doing and you will also become successful. Right?

In reality this is the fastest way to fail and I'm certain it's responsible for the bulk of small business failures. Here are the two major reasons why…

#1 Large Companies Have A Different Agenda

Large companies have a very different agenda when it comes to marketing than small businesses do. Their strategies and priorities differ from yours significantly.

The marketing priorities of a large company looks something like this:

1. Pleasing The Board Of Directors
2. Appeasing Shareholders
3. Satisfying Superiors' Biases
4. Satisfying Existing Clients' Preconceptions
5. Winning Advertising And Creative Awards
6. Getting "Buy In" From Various Committees And Stakeholders
7. Making A Profit

The marketing priorities of a small business owner look something like this:

1. Making A Profit

As you can see there is a world of difference in the marketing priorities of small and large companies. So naturally there would have to be a world of difference in strategy and execution.

#2 Large Companies Have A VERY Different Budget

Strategy changes with scale. This is very important to understand. Do you think someone investing in and building skyscrapers has a different property investment strategy than the average small property investor? Of course.

Using the same strategy simply won't work on a small scale. You can't just build one floor of a skyscraper and have a success. You need all 100 stories.

If you have an advertising budget of $10 million and three years to get a profitable result, then you're going to use a very different strategy compared to someone needing to make a profit immediately with a $10,000 budget.

Using a large company marketing strategy, your $10,000 is going to be a drop in the ocean. It will be totally wasted and ineffective because you're using the wrong strategy for the scale that you're operating at.

Large Company Marketing

Large company marketing is also sometimes known as mass marketing or "branding." The goal of this type of advertising is to remind customers and prospects about your brand as well as the products and services you offer.

The idea is that the more times you run ads from your brand, the more likely people are to have this brand at the top of their consciousness when they go to make a purchasing decision.

The vast majority of large company marketing falls into this category. If you've seen the ads from major brands such as Coca-Cola, Nike and Apple you'll have experienced mass marketing.

This type of marketing is effective; however, it is very expensive to successfully pull off and takes a lot of time. It requires you to saturate various types of advertising media e.g. TV, print, radio, Internet, etc., on a very regular basis and over an extended period of time.

The expense and time involved are not a problem for the major brands as they have massive advertising budgets, teams of marketing people and product lines are planned years in advance.

However, a major problem arises when small businesses try to imitate the big brands at this type of marketing.

The few times they run their ads is like a drop in the ocean. It's nowhere near enough to reach the consciousness of their target market who are bombarded with thousands of marketing messages each day. So they get drowned out and see little or no return for their investment. Another advertising victim bites the dust.

It's not that the small businesses aren't good at "branding" or mass media ads. It's that they simply don't have the budget to run their ads in sufficient volume to make them effective.

Unless you have millions of dollars in your marketing budget, you have a very high probability of failure with this type of marketing.

Branding, mass marketing and ego-based marketing is the domain of large companies. To achieve any kind of cut through requires an enormous budget and the use of expensive mass media.

Following the path of other successful businesses is smart, but it's vital that you understand the full strategy you're following and that you're able to execute it.

Strategy from an outside observer's perspective can be very different to the reality. If you're following a strategy that has different priorities to you or has a vastly different budget then it's highly unlikely it will generate the kind of result you're hoping for.

Now let's look at what successful small to medium business marketing looks like.

Small and Medium Business Marketing

Direct response marketing is a particular branch of marketing that gives small businesses cut through and a competitive edge on a small budget. It's designed to ensure you get a return on investment that is measurable.

If $10 bills were being sold for $2 each, how many would you buy? As many as you could get hands on naturally! The name of the game with direct response marketing is "money at a discount." For example for every $2 spent on advertising, you get $10 out in the way of profits from sales.

It's also a highly ethical way of selling. It's focused on the specific problems of the prospect and aims to solve these problems with education and specific solutions. It is also the only real way for a small business to affordably reach the consciousness of a prospect.

When you turn your ads into direct response ads, they become lead generating tools rather than just name recognition tools.

Direct response marketing is designed to evoke an immediate response and compel prospects to take some specific action, such as opting-in to your email list, picking up the phone and calling for more information, placing an order or being directed to a web page. So what makes a direct response ad? Here are some of the main characteristics:

It's trackable. That is, when someone responds, you know which ad and which media was responsible for generating the response. This is in direct contrast to mass media or "brand" marketing—no one will ever know what ad compelled you to buy that can of Coke, heck you may not even know yourself.

It's measurable. Since you know which ads are being responded to and how many sales you've received from each one, you can measure exactly how effective each ad is. You then drop or change ads that are not giving you a return on investment.

It uses compelling headlines and sales copy. Direct response marketing has a compelling message of strong interest to your chosen prospects. It uses attention-grabbing headlines with strong sales copy that is "salesmanship in print." Often the ad looks more like an editorial than an ad (hence making it at least three times more likely to get read).

It targets a specific audience or niche. Prospects within specific verticals, geographic zones or niche markets are targeted. The ad aims to appeal to a narrow target market.

It makes a specific offer. Usually the ad makes a specific value-packed offer. Often the aim is not necessarily to sell anything from the ad but to simply get the prospect to take the next action, such as requesting a free report. The offer focuses on the prospect rather than on the advertiser and talks about the prospect's interests, desires, fears and frustrations. By contrast, mass media or "brand" marketing has a broad, one-size-fits-all marketing message and is focused on the advertiser.

It demands a response. Direct response advertising has a "call to action," compelling the prospect to do something specific. It also includes a means of response and "capture" of these responses. Interested, high probability prospects have easy ways to respond such as a regular phone number, a free recorded message line, a website, a fax back form, a reply card or coupons. When the prospect responds, as much of the person's contact information as possible is captured so that they can be contacted beyond the initial response.

Multi-step, short-term follow-up. In exchange for capturing the prospect's details, valuable education and information on the prospect's problem is offered. The information should carry with it a second "irresistible offer"—tied to whatever next step you want the prospect to take, such as calling to schedule an appointment or coming into the showroom or store. Then a series of follow-up "touches" via different media such as mail, e-mail, fax, and phone are made. Often there is a time or quantity limit on the offer.

Maintenance follow-up of unconverted leads. People who do not respond within the short-term follow-up period may have many reasons for not "maturing" into buyers immediately. There is value in this bank of slow-to-mature prospects. They should be nurtured and continue hearing from you regularly.

Direct response marketing is a very deep topic with many facets. The 1-Page Marketing Plan is a tool that helps you implement direct response marketing in your business without needing to spend years studying to become an expert.

It's a guided process that helps you create the key elements of a direct response campaign for your business quickly and easily.

The 1-Page Marketing Plan

The 1-Page Marketing Plan template is designed so that you can fill it in, in point form as you read this book and end up with a personalized marketing plan for your business. Here's what a blank template of the 1-Page Marketing Plan looks like:

	1. My Target Market	2. My Message To My Target Market	3. The Media I Will Use To Reach My Target Market
Before (Prospect)			
	4. My Lead Capture System	5. My Lead Nurturing System	6. My Sales Conversion Strategy
During (Lead)			
	7. How I Deliver A World Class Experience	8. How I Increase Customer Lifetime Value	9. How I Orchestrate And Stimulate Referrals
After (Customer)			

There are nine squares split up into the three major phases of the marketing process. Most great plays, movies and books are split up into a three-act structure and so too is good marketing. Let's take a look into these three "acts."

Download your copy of the 1-Page Marketing Plan template at 1pmp.com

The Three Phases Of The Marketing Journey

The marketing process is a journey we want to guide our ideal target market through. We want to guide them from not knowing we exist right through to being a raving fan customer.

Through this journey there are three distinct phases that we guide them through. These phases are the **Before, During** and **After**[2] phases of your marketing process. The following is a brief overview of each of these phases.

Before

We label people going through the before phase as a **prospects**. At the beginning of the "before" phase, prospects typically don't even know you exist. The successful completion of this phase results in the prospect knowing who you are and indicating interest.

Example: Tom is a busy business owner and is frustrated that he can't keep his contacts in sync between his laptop and smartphone. He searches online for a solution and comes across an ad with the headline "Five Little Known Strategies That Unlock The Power Of Your Business IT System." Tom clicks on the ad and is taken to an online form where he must enter his email address in order to download a free report. Tom sees value in what the report has to offer so enters his email address.

During

We label people going through the during phase as a **leads**. At the beginning of the "during" phase, leads have indicated some interest in your offer. The successful completion of this phase results in the prospect buying from you for the first time.

Example: Tom gets a lot of value from the report he downloaded. It has some genuinely good tips that he didn't previously know and

---

[2]   Dean Jackson is a direct response marketing legend and developed the "before, during and after" concept.

21

implementing them has saved him a lot of time. In addition, the IT company that wrote the report has been emailing him additional valuable tips and information and offers Tom a free Twenty-one-point IT audit for his business. Tom takes them up on this offer. The audit is thorough and professional and reveals to Tom that his IT systems are vulnerable because a lot of the software on his computers is out of date. Also, the backups he thought were happening actually stopped working six months ago. They offer Tom a heavily discounted offer where they'll send a technician to fix all the problems identified during the audit. Tom takes them up on this offer.

After

We label people in this phase as **customers**[3]. At the beginning of the "after" phase, customers have already given you money. The after never ends and when executed correctly, results in a virtuous cycle where the customer buys from you repeatedly and is such a fan of your products or services that they consistently recommend you and introduce you to new prospects.

Example: Tom is extremely impressed with the professionalism of the technician that came in and fixed his IT problems. The technician was on time, courteous and explained everything to Tom in plain English. Importantly, he follows through on his company's promise of "Fixed First Time or It's Free." Someone from headquarters follows up with Tom the next day to ensure he's satisfied with the service he received. Tom indicates that he is very satisfied. During this follow-up call, Tom is offered a maintenance package where a qualified technician will look after his IT systems for a fixed monthly fee. It also includes unlimited technical support so if Tom is stuck at any time, he can call a toll free number and get immediate help. Tom takes up this offer. The support line alone is of huge value to him as he frequently gets frustrated with his IT system and loses productive time trying to figure out a fix.

---

[3] We use the label 'customer' as a generic term for people that pay you money. Depending on what type of business you're in, this label could be customer, client, or patient.

Tom even refers three of his business friends from his golf club to this company because of the great service he's experienced.

In summary if we were to describe the three phases in table form, it would look like this:

Phase	Status	Goal Of This Phase
Before	Prospect	Get them to **know you** and indicate interest
During	Lead	Get them to **like you** and buy from you for the first time
After	Customer	Get them to **trust you** and buy from you regularly and refer

Now that we've got a good bird's eye view of the overall structure, it's time to dive in and look in depth at each of the nine squares that make up your 1-Page Marketing Plan.

Important: Download your copy of the 1-Page Marketing Plan template at 1pmp.com

ACT I

The "Before" Phase

The "Before" Phase Section Summary

In the "before" phase you're dealing with prospects. Prospects are people that may not even yet know you exist. In this phase you'll identify a target market, craft a compelling message for this target market and deliver your message to them through advertising media.

The goal of this phase is to get your prospect to know you and respond to your message. Once they've indicated interest by responding, they become a lead and enter the second phase of your marketing process.

Chapter 1

Selecting Your Target Market

Chapter 1 Summary

Selecting your target market is a crucial first step in the marketing process. Doing so will ensure your marketing message resonates better, which in turn will make your marketing far more effective. By focusing on the right target market for your business, you'll be able to get a better return on the time, money and energy you invest.

Highlights covered in this chapter include:

- Why targeting everyone with your product or service is a terrible idea.
- Why mass marketing can be harmful to your business and cost you far more than it makes you.
- How to use the "PVP index" to select your perfect target market.
- Why you should focus on a niche and become a big fish in a small pond.
- How to make price irrelevant.
- Why you should stop advertising a long list of products and services.
- How to go deep into the mind of your prospect so you can understand exactly what they want.

It's Not Everyone

When I ask business owners who their target market is, many tend to respond with "everyone." In reality this means no one. In their zeal to acquire as many customers as possible, many business owners try to serve the widest market possible.

On the face it of it this seems logical. However, it's actually a huge mistake. Many business owners worry about narrowing down their target market because they don't want to exclude any potential customers.

This is a typical newbie marketing mistake. In this chapter we're going to examine why excluding customers is actually a good thing.

As discussed in the previous chapter, most large company advertising falls into a category called mass marketing, sometimes also referred to as "branding." With this type of marketing, business owners are like an archer in the middle of a dense fog, shooting arrows in every direction in the hope that one or more of them will hit the intended target.

The theory behind mass marketing is that you want to "get your name out there." I'm not really sure exactly where "there" is or what's supposed to happen when your name arrives "there." Regardless the theory is that if you broadcast your message enough times, you'll by chance get an audience with your prospects and some percentage of them will buy from you.

If that sounds a lot like our disoriented archer, flailing about in the fog, shooting his arrows in random directions and hoping for the best, then you'd be right. However, you might be thinking—if he just shoots enough arrows in all directions, surely he's bound to hit his target. Right? Maybe, but for small to medium sized businesses at least, that's the stupid way of marketing because they'll never have enough arrows (i.e., money) to hit their target enough times to get a good return on their investment.

To be a successful small business marketer you need laser-like focus on a narrow target market, sometimes called a niche.

Niching—Harnesses The Power Of Focus

Before going any further let's define what a business niche is.

A niche is a tightly defined portion of a subcategory. For example think of the health and beauty category. This is a very wide category. A beauty salon can offer a wide variety of services including tanning, waxing, facials, massage, cellulite treatment and much more. If, for example, we take one of these subcategories—let's say cellulite treatment, this could be our niche. However, we could tighten it up even further by focusing on cellulite treatment for women who've just had a baby. This is a tightly defined niche. Now you may be thinking why on earth would we want to limit our market so much? Here's why:

1. You have a limited amount of money. If you focus too broadly, your marketing message will become diluted and weak.
2. The other critical factor is relevance. The goal of your ad is for your prospects to say, "Hey that's for me."

If you're a woman who's just had a baby and are concerned about cellulite, would an ad targeting this specific problem grab your interest? Most certainly. How about if the ad was a general ad for a beauty salon which reeled off a long list of services, one of which was cellulite treatment? Likely it would get missed in the clutter.

A 100 watt light bulb, like the kind of light bulb we normally have in our homes, lights up a room. By contrast a 100 watt laser can cut through steel. Same energy, dramatically different result. The difference being how the energy is focused. The exact same thing is true of your marketing.

Take another example of a photographer. If you look at ads from most photographers you'll often see a laundry list of services like:

- Portraits
- Weddings
- Family photography
- Commercial photography

- Fashion photography
- etc.

The technical way photography is done may not change very much from situation to situation, but let me ask you a question. Do you think someone looking for wedding photography would respond to a different ad than someone who's after commercial photography?

Do you think a bride-to-be looking for a photographer for her special day might be looking for something radically different than a purchasing manager from a heavy machinery distributor looking to photograph a truck for a product brochure? Of course.

However, if the ad just rolls out a broad laundry list of services, then it's not speaking to either prospect, therefore it's not relevant, therefore it will likely be ignored by both market segments.

That's why you need to choose a narrow target market for your marketing campaign.

Being all things to all people leads to marketing failure. This doesn't mean you can't offer a broad range of services, but understand that each category of service is a separate campaign.

Targeting a tight niche allows you to become a big fish in a small pond. It allows you to dominate a category or geography in a way that is impossible by being general.

The type of niches that you want to go after are "an inch wide and a mile deep." An inch wide meaning it is a very highly targeted subsection of a category. A mile deep meaning there's a lot of people looking for a solution to that specific problem. Once you dominate one niche, you can expand your business by finding another profitable and highly targeted niche, then dominate that one also.

Now you can have all the advantages of being highly targeted without limiting the potential size of your business.

Niching Makes Price Irrelevant

If you had just suffered a heart attack, would you prefer to be treated by a general doctor or a heart specialist? Of course you'd choose the specialist. Now if you had a consultation with the heart specialist, would you expect them to charge you more than a general doctor? Of course.

Your bill with the specialist would likely be much higher than with your general practitioner, yet you're not shopping on price.

How did price suddenly become irrelevant? That is the beauty of serving a niche. Whether you do heart surgery or offer cellulite treatment, you can now charge far more for your services than by being a generalist. You're perceived differently by your prospects and customers. A specialist is sought after, rather than shopped on price. A specialist is much more highly respected than a jack of all trades. A specialist is paid handsomely to solve a specific problem for their target market.

So figure out the one thing your market wants a solution to, something that they'll pay you handsomely for. Then enter the conversation they're having in their mind, preferably something they go to bed worrying about and wake up thinking about. Do this and your results will dramatically improve.

Trying to target everyone in reality means you're targeting no one. By going too broad you kill your "specialness" and become a commodity bought on price. By narrowly defining a target market that you can wow and deliver huge results for, you become a specialist.

When you narrow down your target market, you naturally decide who you're going to exclude. Don't underestimate the importance of this. Excluding potential customers scares many small business owners. They mistakenly believe that a wider net is more likely to capture more customers. This is a huge mistake. Dominate a niche, then once you own it, do the same with another and then another. But never do so all at once. Doing so dilutes your message and your marketing power.

How To Identify Your Ideal Customer

Given that you've now seen the power of choosing a narrow target market it's time to select yours. As with most businesses, you may currently serve multiple market segments. For example back to our photographer friend, he might do:

- Weddings
- Corporate photography
- Photojournalism
- Family portraits

These are vastly different market segments. A great way of figuring out your **ideal** target market is to use the PVP index[4] (**P**ersonal fulfillment, **V**alue to the marketplace and **P**rofitability) and giving each market segment you serve a rating out of 10.

P - Personal fulfillment: How much do you enjoy dealing with this type of customer? Sometimes we work with "pain in the butt" type customers just because of the money. Here you rate how much you enjoy working with this market segment.

V - Value To The Marketplace: How much does this market segment value your work? Are they willing to pay you a lot of $$$ for your work?

P - Profitability: How profitable is the work you do for this market segment? Sometimes even when you are charging high fees for your work, when you look at the numbers it may be barely profitable or even loss making. Remember it's not about the "turnover," it's all about the "left over."

For our photographer example, his PVP index may look as follows:

Weddings: Personal fulfillment = 5 Value to the marketplace = 7 Profits = 9 Total score: 21	**Photojournalism:** Personal fulfillment = 9 Value to the marketplace = 7 Profits = 2 Total score: 18
Corporate photography: Personal fulfillment = 3 Value to the marketplace = 6 Profits = 9 Total score: 18	**Family portraits:** Personal fulfillment = 9 Value to the marketplace = 8 Profits = 9 Total score: 26

---

[4] The PVP concept is one I shamelessly stole from Frank Kern.

The **ideal** customer for the photographer is people wanting family portraits. They are the most fun, most profitable, highest value and best paying types of customers. There's likely to be a standout market segment for you too.

This doesn't mean that you can't take on work outside your ideal target market; however, for now our marketing efforts will be directed at one **ideal** market segment. We want to be laser focused. Once we dominate this market segment, we can go on and add others. If we are too broad initially and target a laundry list of market segments, then our marketing efforts will be ineffective.

Who is your ideal target market? Be as specific as possible about all the attributes that may be relevant. What is their gender, age, geography?

Do you have a picture of them? If so, cut out or print a picture of them when you think about and answer the following questions:

What keeps them awake at night, indigestion boiling up their esophagus, eyes open, staring at the ceiling?

What are they afraid of?

What are they angry about?

Who are they angry at?

What are their top daily frustrations?

What trends are occurring and will occur in their businesses or lives?

What do they secretly, ardently desire most?

Is there a built-in bias to the way they make decisions? (Example: engineers = exceptionally analytical)

Do they have their own language or jargon they use?

What magazines do they read?

What websites do they visit?

What's this person's day like?

What's the main dominant emotion this market feels?

What is the ONE thing they crave above all else?

These questions are not theoretical, pie-in-the-sky questions. They are absolutely key to your marketing success. Unless you can get into the mind of your prospect, all your other marketing efforts will be wasted—no matter how well you execute.

Unless you belong to your target market, then a large part of your initial marketing efforts should be directed to in-depth research, interviews and careful study of your target market.

Create An Avatar

One of the best tools for getting into the mind of your prospect is to temporarily become them by creating an avatar. Don't worry, I'm not going to get all woo woo on you here.

An avatar is a detailed exploration and description of your target customer and their lives. Like a police sketch artist you piece together a composite which creates a vivid picture of them in your mind. It helps tell their story so that you can visualize life from their perspective.

It's also important to create avatars for each type of decision maker or influencer you might encounter in your target market. For example if you're selling IT services to small companies in the financial services industry you might be dealing with both the business owner and their assistant.

Here's an example of avatars for Max Cash, the owner of a successful financial planning firm and his personal assistant Angela Assistant.

Max Cash:

Max is 51 years old.

He owns a successful financial planning business which has grown steadily over the past ten years. Previously, he had a career working for KPMG and some other large corporates before he went out on his own.

He has a bachelor's degree and an MBA.

He's married has two teenage daughters and younger son.

He lives in an upper-middle-class suburb in a five-bedroom house which he's been in for about four years. He drives a two-year-old Mercedes S-Class.

He has eighteen staff members and operates from an office building which he owns. His office is a fifteen-minute drive from home.

The business has an annual turnover of $4.5M which is predominantly service-based revenue.

He has no IT support person on staff and delegates most of the IT and tech responsibilities to his PA, Angela Assistant.

He spends about four thousand dollars per month on the various pieces of software used in his industry which give him access to the most current financial data. He knows the software helps him and his clients but he also knows that there are many features that are going underutilized.

His office server and systems are a hodgepodge of various computers mostly installed by his software vendors and which have had very little maintenance since installation. The backup systems are archaic and have never actually been tested.

He's a golf nut. His office is decorated with golf memorabilia. There are photos of him playing golf throughout. The desktop background on his computer is a beautiful panoramic photo of Pebble Beach Golf Links.

In his spare time, unsurprisingly, he likes to play golf with his friends and business associates.

He reads *The Wall Street Journal, Bloomberg Businessweek* and his local newspaper.

He uses an iPhone but it's mostly used for phone calls and a little bit of email.

See how this can give us a valuable insight into what the life of our prospect looks like? Now let's look at the avatar for another influencer within our target market:

Angela Assistant:

Angela is 29 years old.

She's single and lives in a two-bedroom rented apartment with her cat Sprinkles. She takes public transport to work and commutes daily for about thirty minutes.

Angela is organized, always smartly dressed and very enthusiastic.

Angela has been working for Max as his PA for the last three years when the growth of the company had really started to accelerate. She's his right hand and he'd be totally lost without her.

She organizes Max's calendar, sets up his laptop and phone, makes and takes calls on his behalf and much, much more. She's the glue that holds Max's business together and she does a bit of everything from ordering stationary to IT to HR.

Although her title says PA, she's more than that. She's really the office manager and probably even to some extent the general manager. She's the one that staff go to when something needs to be fixed, ordered or organized.

She's tech savvy but really out of her depth when it comes to the more technical and strategic aspects of IT systems.

After work, she usually hits the gym for a workout and loves to watch new shows on Netflix. On weekends she catches up with friends and loves the nightlife.

She spends a lot of time online reading beauty, fashion and celebrity gossip blogs.

Angela spends most of her discretionary income on going out, entertainment and online shopping which is like an addiction for her. Even though Angela is quite well paid, she always runs short of money, which has resulted in her having about $10,000 worth of credit card debt. She knows she needs to be better with money but there always just seems to be too many temptations for her to resist.

She's always glued to her phone, constantly texting and using social media apps.

To take a step further, find an actual image to visually represent your avatar and have it in front of you whenever you're creating marketing material for them.

Hopefully by now you can see how powerful avatars are. They are the marketing equivalent of method acting. They get you right into the mind of your prospect which is going to be absolutely crucial when it comes to crafting your message to your target market.

Chapter 1 Action Item:
Who Is Your Target Market?
Fill in square #1 of your 1-Page Marketing Plan

Chapter 2

Crafting Your Message

Chapter 2 Summary

Most marketing messages are boring, timid and ineffective. To stand out from the crowd you need to craft a compelling message that grabs the attention of your target market. Once you have their attention, the goal of your message is to compel them to respond.

Highlights covered in this chapter include:

- Why most advertising is totally useless and what to do instead.
- How to stand out from the crowd even when you're selling a commodity.
- Why you should never compete solely on price.
- How to craft a compelling offer for your target market.
- Examples of some of the most successful advertising headlines in history.
- How to enter the mind of your prospect and join the conversation going on in there.
- How to effectively name your business, product or service.

An Accident Waiting To Happen

I spend a lot of time looking through various forms of local and national media—not for articles but for advertisements. Having done this for several years, with very few exceptions, I'm absolutely amazed how boring, similar and useless most advertising is. The waste going on is staggering. Wasted money and wasted opportunity.

You could summarize the structure of most ads from small businesses as follows:

- Company name
- Company logo
- A laundry list of services offered
- Claims of best quality, best service or best prices
- Offer of a "free quote"
- Contact details

It's basically name, rank and serial number. Then they hope and pray that on the very day their ad runs, a prospect in immediate need of their product or service stumbles across it and takes action. This is what I call marketing by accident. A qualified prospect happening upon the right ad at the right time sometimes results in the happy accident of a sale taking place.

If these "accidents" never happened then no one would ever advertise. But as it happens the occasional random sale or lead will come from this type of advertising. It tortures business owners to death because while the ad generally loses them money, they fear not running it because some dribs and drabs of new business have come out of it—and who knows, next week it may bring in that big sale they've been hoping for.

It's like these businesses are visiting a slot machine in a casino. They put their money in, pull the handle and hope for a jackpot—but most of the time the house just takes their money. Occasionally they'll get a few cents on the dollar back which raises their hopes and emboldens them to continue.

It's time to start marketing on purpose—treating advertising like a vending machine where the results and value generated are predictable, rather than like a slot machine where the results are random and the odds are stacked against you.

[handwritten: very hard one]

To start marketing on purpose we need to look at two vital elements:

1. What Is The Purpose Of Your Ad?
2. What Does Your Ad Focus On?

When I ask business owners what the purpose of their ad is, I usually get a list like:

- Branding
- Getting my name out there
- Letting people know about my products and services
- Making sales
- Getting people to call in for a quote

These are all very different and you cannot possibly do all of these with one ad. In typical small business style they're trying to get maximum bang for their buck. But by trying to do too much, they end up achieving none of their objectives.

My rule of thumb is one ad, one objective. If something in the ad isn't helping you achieve that objective then it's detracting from it and you should get rid of it. That includes sacred cows like your company name and company logo. Advertising space is valuable and these things taking up prime real estate in your ad space often detract from your message rather than enhance it.

Rather than trying to sell directly from your ad, simply invite prospects to put their hand up and indicate interest. This lowers resistance and helps you build a marketing database—one of the most valuable assets in your business.

Once your objective is clear, you need to communicate it to your reader. What exactly do you want them to do next? Do they call your toll free number to order? Do they call you or visit your website to request a free sample? Do they request a free report? You need a very clear call to action—not something wimpy and vague like "don't hesitate to call us."

[handwritten: Weak - indefinitely]

You need to be clear on what they should do next and what they will get in return. Also, give them multiple ways to take that action. For example if the call to action is to order your product, give them the ability to do it online, over the phone or even via a mail-in coupon. Different people have different preferences when it comes to modality of communication. Give them multiple means of response so they can choose the one they are most comfortable with.

Have you ever been to a party or gathering and been seated next to someone who just spends the whole night talking about themselves? It gets old pretty fast. You keep giving halfhearted smiles and polite nods but your mind is elsewhere and that exit sign is calling your name.

Similarly, most advertising by small businesses is inwardly focused. Instead of speaking to the needs and problems of the prospect, it is focused on self-aggrandizement. The prominent logo and company name, the laundry list of services, the claims of being the leading provider of that product or service. All of these things are shouting, "look at me!"

Unfortunately, you're in a crowded market and with everyone shouting "look at me!" at the same time, it just becomes background noise. By contrast, direct response marketing focuses heavily on the needs, thoughts and emotions of the target market. By doing this you enter the conversation already going on in the mind of your ideal prospect. You will resonate at a deeper level with your prospect and your ad will stand out from 99% of other ads that are just shouting and talking about themselves.

Don't be the advertising equivalent of that guy at the party obliviously talking about himself the whole night while his uninterested audience looks for the exit. Also, don't leave anything to chance. Know exactly what you want your ad to achieve and the exact action you want your prospect to take.

Developing A Unique Selling Proposition

Many small businesses don't have a reason to exist. Take away their name and logo from their website or other marketing material and you'd never know who they were. They could be any of the other businesses in their category. Their reason for existence is to survive and pay the bills of the owner who is usually only just getting by or possibly not even.

From a customer's perspective, there is no compelling reason to buy from them and any sales they do make is just because they happen to be there. You see a lot of these businesses in retail. The only sales they get is through random walk-in traffic. No one is seeking them out. No one actively desires what they have to offer and if they weren't there no one would miss them. Harsh but true.

The problem is that these businesses are just another "me too" business. How did they decide on price? How did they decide on product? How did they decide on marketing? Usually the answer is they just had a look at what their nearest competitor was doing and did the same thing or slightly changed something. Don't get me wrong, there's nothing wrong in modeling something that's already working. In fact that's a very smart thing to do. However, it's likely the competitors they are modeling are in the same boat they are in—struggling to win business with no compelling reason why you should buy from them. They based their most important business decisions on guesses and on what their mediocre competitors are doing. It's the blind leading the blind.

After some time of torturing themselves to death—making just enough money to survive but not enough money to do well, many of these businesses finally decide to "try marketing." So they start marketing their "me too" business with an equally boring "me too" message. As expected, it doesn't work and any extra sales it does bring in often doesn't even cover the marketing costs.

Here's the thing—the chance of you getting your marketing perfectly right—message to market and media match on the first go is impossibly small. Even the most experienced marketer will tell you they hardly ever hit a homerun on their first go. It takes several iterations. It takes testing and measuring to finally get your message to market and media match right.

Yet these guys can't afford the time, money and effort needed to get it right. Worse still with a "me too" style of offer they don't have a hope.

Think of marketing as an amplifier. Here's an example. You tell one person about what you do and they don't get excited. You then try telling ten people about what you do and they don't get excited either. If you amplify this message through marketing and tell 10,000 people, what makes you think that the result will be any different?

Marketing is an uphill battle if you haven't clearly clarified first in your mind why your business exists and why people should buy from you rather than your nearest competitor.

You need to develop your **unique selling proposition** (USP). This is where a lot of people get stuck. They say something like "I sell coffee, there's nothing unique about that."

Really? Then why aren't we all just getting our $1 coffee from 7-Eleven? Why do we queue up to spend $4 to $5 to buy our coffee from some hipster that looks like he's in urgent need of a bath? Think about it. You regularly pay 400%-500% more for the same commodity.

Think about water—one of the most abundant commodities on earth. When you buy this commodity, in bottled form at either a convenience store or from a vending machine, you happily pay 2000 times the price compared to getting it from your tap at home.

See how the commodity in both examples hasn't changed, but the circumstances and things around the commodity have changed or the way they are packaged and delivered has changed?

The entire goal of your USP is to answer this question: **Why should I buy from you rather than from your nearest competitor?**

Another good test is this: if I removed the company name and logo from your website, would people still know that it's you or could it be any other company in your industry?

The common place that people go wrong with developing their USP is they say "quality" or "great service" is their USP. There are two things wrong with that:

1. Quality and great service are expectations, they are just part of good business practice—not something unique.
2. People only find out about your quality and great service **after** they've bought. A good USP is designed to attract prospects **before** they've made a purchasing decision.

You know you're marketing your business as a commodity when prospects start the conversation by asking you about price.

Positioning yourself as a commodity and hence being shopped on price alone is a terrible position for a small business owner to be in. It's soul crushing and this race to the bottom is bound to end in tears.

The answer is to develop a unique selling proposition (USP). Something that positions you differently, so that prospects are forced to make an apples-to-oranges comparison when comparing you with your competitor.

If they can do an apples-to-apples comparison of you and your competitors then it comes down to price and you're toast. There's always someone willing to sell cheaper than you.

There's Nothing New Under The Sun

Very few if any businesses or products are truly unique, so a common question is, "There's nothing unique about my business, how do I develop a USP?"

There are two questions I ask my clients when helping them develop their USP. Answering these two questions is the path towards marketing and financial success in your business.

So the two questions you must ask and answer are:

- Why should they buy?
- Why should they buy from me?

These are questions that should have clear, concise and quantifiable answers. Not wishy-washy nonsense like "we are the best" or "we have the highest quality."

What is the unique advantage you are offering? Now the uniqueness doesn't have to be in the product itself. In fact, it would be fair to say that there are very few truly unique products. The uniqueness may be in the way it is packaged, delivered, supported or even sold.

You need to position what you do in such a way that even if your competitor was operating directly opposite you, customers would cross the road to do business with you instead of your competitor.

Do it really well and they may even stand in line overnight to do business with you instead of your competitor, like they do with Apple products.

Getting Into The Mind Of Your Prospect

We want to get into the mind of our prospect. What do they really want? It's rarely the thing you are selling, it's usually the result of the thing you are selling. The difference may seem subtle but it's huge.

For example someone buying a $50 watch is buying something very different from a person buying a $50,000 watch. In the latter case they are likely buying status, luxury and exclusivity. Sure they want it to tell the time just like the buyer of the $50 watch but that's unlikely to be their core motivation.

So to get into the mind of the prospect, we need to discover what result they are actually buying. Once you understand this, you then need to craft your unique selling proposition based on the result your prospects want to achieve.

For example, if you're a printer, you're in a commodity business. You want to get out of the commodity business as quickly as possible. I don't mean get out of the industry but you do need to change how you position yourself.

Stop selling business cards, brochures and printing and start asking open-ended questions such as, "Why are you coming to a printer? What is it that you want to achieve?" The prospect doesn't want business cards and brochures, they want what they think business cards and brochures are going to do for their business.

So you could sit down with them and say, "What are you trying to accomplish? Let's do a printing audit and evaluate all of the things you're trying to use printing for." By taking them through the process, you can charge them to do a printing audit. Then if they end up hiring you to do their printing, you can apply that consulting fee towards printing. This way you're no longer viewed as a printer anymore. You're now viewed as a trusted advisor that's serving their needs.

If You Confuse Them You Lose Them

Understand that your prospect has essentially three options:

- Buy from you
- Buy from your competitor
- Do nothing

You may think your competitors are your biggest problem, but in reality it's more likely to be a fight against inertia. Therefore you need to first answer the question of why they should buy and in addition to why they should buy from YOU.

We live in a sound bite, MTV generation which has to deal with thousands of messages each day. The importance of crafting your message in an immediately understandable and impactful way has never been more important.

Can you explain your product and the unique benefit it offers in a single short sentence?

You must understand a very important concept: confusion leads to lost sales. This is especially so when you have a complex product. Many business owners erroneously think that a confused customer will seek clarification or contact you for more information. Nothing could be further from the truth. **When you confuse them, you lose them**.

People have too many options and too much information coming at them constantly and they're rarely motivated enough to wade through a confused message.

How To Be Remarkable When You Are Selling A Commodity

How do you charge high prices for your products and services while having your customers thank you for it? In short, by being remarkable.

When given this answer, the first thing many business owners do is mutter under their breath something like, "easier said than done"—perhaps it's because being remarkable evokes visions of being unattainably unique or creative. Something that others far more talented do.

The cafe owner says, "dude I just sell coffee, how am I supposed to be remarkable?" That raises a common question, how can you be remarkable when you sell a commodity?

Let's look at a few examples.

When I talk about being remarkable, it doesn't necessarily mean that the product or service you sell is unique. Far from it. In fact being unique is a dangerous, difficult and expensive place to be. However, you must be different. How can our cafe owner be different? Check this out:

How much extra did it cost the cafe to serve art with its coffee? Pretty close to zero I would expect. Maybe some extra training for the barista and a few extra seconds of time per cup.

But how many people will each customer tell or better still bring in to show? Could this cafe owner charge 50¢ more per cup than the cafe down the road? For sure. That's 50¢ of pure profit multiplied by hundreds of thousands of cups per year straight to the bottom line.

Yet is the product unique? Not by a long shot—just slightly different. Different enough to be remarkable.

Here's another example. Most e-commerce sites send the same boring confirmation email when you buy from them. Something along the lines of, "Your order has been shipped. Please let us know if it doesn't arrive. Thank you for your business."

Instead have a look at how CD Baby creates a remarkable experience for the customer and a viral marketing opportunity for themselves instead of a normal boring confirmation email:

Your CD has been gently taken from our CD Baby shelves with sterilized contamination-free gloves and placed onto a satin pillow.

A team of 50 employees inspected your CD and polished it to make sure it was in the best possible condition before mailing.

Our packing specialist from Japan lit a candle and a hush fell over the crowd as he put your CD into the finest gold-lined box that money can buy.

We all had a wonderful celebration afterwards and the whole party marched down the street to the post office where the entire town of Portland waved "Bon Voyage!" to your package, on its way to you, in our private CD Baby jet on this day, Friday, June 6th.

I hope you had a wonderful time shopping at CD Baby. We sure did. Your picture is on our wall as "Customer of the Year." We're all exhausted but can't wait for you to come back to CDBABY.COM!!

This order confirmation email has been forwarded thousands of times and posted on countless blogs and websites. Derek Sivers, the founder of CD Baby credits this remarkable order confirmation message for creating thousands of new customers.

Again nothing unique about the product, but the transformation of something ordinary and boring gives the customer a smile and creates free viral marketing for the business.

One more example from another highly competitive, commodity industry—consumer electronics:

When Apple first launched their legendary music player, the iPod, they could have talked about the five-gigabyte storage capacity or other technical features like all the other music players of the day did. But instead how did they promote it?

"1000 songs in your pocket"

Genius! Five gigabytes doesn't mean a thing to most consumers. Neither does a bunch of technical jargon, but "1000 songs in your pocket"—anyone can instantly understand that and the benefits it will offer.

Apple was by no means the first portable music player on the market or even the best, but they were by far the most successful because of their ability to quickly and easily convey the reasons why you should buy. Notice in all three of the examples the actual product being sold is a commodity and what makes it remarkable is something totally peripheral to what you are buying.

Yet the seller can, and does, command premium pricing because they are selling a remarkable experience. Not only is the customer happy to pay the premium but in fact rewards the seller by spreading the message about their product or service. Why? Because we all want to share things and experiences that are remarkable.

What can you do in your business that's remarkable? Your clarity around this will have a huge impact on the success of your business.

Lowest Price

I'm sometimes asked, "Can't lowest price be my USP?" Sure it can, but can you absolutely guarantee that everything you sell will be priced lower than all your competitors including the behemoths like Costco and Walmart? Unlikely.

There'll always be someone willing to go out of business faster than you. I suggest you not play that game.

So a USP that says "lowest prices on some things, some of the time" is not quite so compelling.

The fact is if you're a small or medium business, you're unlikely to beat the big discounters at the lowest price game.

Truth be told, you probably don't want to. By charging higher prices, you attract a better quality client. As counterintuitive as it may seem, you get far less grief from high-end customers than you do from low-end ones. I've seen and experienced this in multiple businesses across multiple industries.

A better option than discounting is to increase the value of your offering. Bundling in bonuses, adding services, customizing the solution can all be of genuine value to your customer but can cost you very little to do.

This also helps you create that valuable apples-to-oranges comparison that gets you out of the commodity game.

Don't hate the player, hate the game. So as hard as it may be to resist, don't play the commodity/price game. Develop your USP, deliver on it and make those you deal with play your game, on your terms.

Create Your Elevator Pitch

As a business owner, being able to succinctly convey what problem you solve is a real art, especially if you're in a business that is complex.

A great way of distilling your USP is by crafting an "elevator pitch." An elevator pitch is a concise, well-rehearsed summary of your business and its value proposition which can be delivered in the time span of an elevator ride, i.e. 30-90 seconds.

Yes it's cheesy and you may not even really use it often as an elevator pitch but it can really help you clarify your message and your USP. This will become extremely valuable when you get to crafting your offer, which we'll cover shortly.

The thirty seconds that follows the "what do you do?" question is one of the most commonly wasted marketing opportunities. The response is almost always self-focused, unclear and often nonsensical.

This is where many people reply with the highest-sounding title they can get away with, as they feel the inquirer's judgment of their worth will depend on the answer. "I'm a waste management technician," says the janitor.

I once asked a lady what she did for a living to which she replied, "I'm a senior event builder." None the wiser about what she did, I continued probing until I finally came to understand that she arranges seating for concerts and large events in stadiums.

While it's true some shallow people judge a person's worth by their job title or line of business, there's a much better way to respond to this question. A way that doesn't require you to raid a thesaurus in order to inflate or obfuscate what you really do.

The next time someone asks what you do for a living, it's your queue to deliver an elevator pitch. It's a perfect opportunity to convey your marketing message on a regular basis and in many different settings.

Obviously, you don't want to come across as a pushy, obnoxious salesperson, so it's important to structure your elevator pitch properly. Most elevator pitches suffer from the same problem as overinflated job titles. It leaves the recipient confused or thinking "what a douchebag" rather than the intended effect of impressing them.

Bad marketing is highly product-focused and self-focused. Good marketing, especially direct response marketing, is always customer and problem/solution focused, and that's exactly how we want our elevator pitch to be. We want to be remembered for what problem we solve rather than for some impressive but incomprehensible title or business.

Good marketing takes the prospect through a journey that covers the problem, the solution and finally the proof. Your elevator pitch should be no different.

So how do you effectively communicate these three components in the space of thirty or so seconds? The best formula I've seen is:

You know [problem]? Well what we do is [solution]. In fact [proof].

Here are a few of examples:

Insurance Sales: *"You know how most people rarely review their insurance coverage when their circumstances change? Well what I do is help people have peace of mind by ensuring their insurance coverage always matches their current circumstances. In fact, just last week a client of mine was robbed, but he was able to recover the full cost of the items he'd lost because his insurance coverage was up to date."*

Electrical Engineering: *"You know when there are power outages that bring down critical systems in large businesses? Well what I do is install backup power systems for companies that rely on having a continual supply of power for their operations. In fact, I installed the system at XYZ Bank which has resulted in them having 100% uptime since the system was installed."*

Website Development: *"You know how most company websites are out of date? Well what I do is install software that makes it easy for people to update their own websites, without the need to pay a web designer each time. In fact, I installed the software for one of my clients recently and they saved $2,000 a year in web development costs."*

This gives you a reliable formula to craft your elevator pitch while being customer/problem focused rather than you/product focused.

Crafting Your Offer

This part is absolutely crucial and this is where a lot of people get lazy by offering something boring, price discounting or copying what their nearest competitor is doing.

Remember if you don't give your ideal target market a reason why your offer is different, they will default to price as the main criteria for making their decision. After all if vendor A is selling apples for $1 and vendor B is selling the same apples for $1.50 which would you buy based on the information you have on hand?

It's your job to create an offer that is exciting and radically different from that of your competitors.

Two great questions to think about when you're crafting your offer are:

1. Of all the products and services you offer, which do you have the most confidence in delivering? For example, if you only got paid if the client achieved their desired result, what product or service would you offer? Phrasing it another way—what problem are you sure that you could solve for a member of your target market?

2. Of all the products and services you offer, which do you enjoy delivering the most?

Some supplemental questions that can help you craft your offer include:

- What is my target market really buying? (e.g. people don't really buy insurance, they buy peace of mind)
- What's the biggest benefit to lead with?
- What are the best emotionally charged words and phrases that will capture and hold the attention of this market?
- What objections do my prospects have and how will I solve them?
- What outrageous offer (including a guarantee) can we make?
- Is there an intriguing story we can tell?

- Who else is selling something similar to my product or service, and how?
- Who else has tried selling them something similar, and how has that effort failed?

One of the main reasons marketing campaigns fail is because the offer is lazy and poorly thought out. It's something crappy and unexciting like 10% or 20% off.

The offer is one of the most important parts of your marketing campaign and you need to spend much of your time and energy on structuring this correctly.

What Does My Target Market Want?

Putting the right stuff in front of the wrong people or the wrong stuff in front of the right people is one of the first marketing mistakes made by business owners.

That's why the first and arguably most important square of the 1-Page Marketing Plan is all about identifying a specific target market for our marketing efforts.

Now that we've laid that groundwork, we want to structure an offer that will excite this target market. One that will have them ready to whip out their wallet and one that will stand out from all the boring, lazy offers from our competitors.

One of the easiest methods of finding out what your prospects want is simply by asking them. You can do so through a survey or through more formal market research.

It should also be noted that most people don't know what they want until they've actually been presented with it. Also when people are doing surveys or responding to market research, they do so with logic; **however, when it comes to actual purchasing, this is done with emotions and justified with logic after the fact**. So you need to supplement asking with observing.

If you asked those in the market for expensive luxury cars as to what they wanted, you'd typically get logical (and untrue or half true) answers like quality, reliability, comfort. In reality what they really want is status. A quote often attributed to Henry Ford puts it well:

> *"If I had asked people what they wanted, they would have said faster horses."*

One of the ways I've done and recommend doing market research is by analyzing what your target market are actually buying or looking for.

Look at products and categories that are trending on marketplaces like Amazon and Ebay.

Analyzing search engine queries can be a great using a tool like Google's Adwords Keyword Tool is another method.

Lastly see what topics are trending on social media and industry news sites. What are people commenting on and reacting to?

Using these tools is almost like tapping into the global consciousness and will give you a good idea of what is currently in demand and being talked or thought about.

Create An Irresistible Offer

Now that you know what your market wants, you need to package it up and present it as an irresistible offer. Here are some of the essential elements:

Value: First you need to think, what is the most valuable thing you could do for your customer? What is the result which takes them from point A to point B that you can take them through while making a good profit?

This really is the crux of your offer.

Language: If you're not a member of your target market, you need to learn the language and jargon used within your target market. If you're selling BMX bikes you need talk about "endos," "sick wheelies" and "bunny hops," not features, benefits and specifications. If you're selling golf clubs you need to talk about "hooks," "slices" and "handicaps."

Reason Why: When you have a great offer, you need to justify why you're doing this. People are so used to being shortchanged that when someone makes a strong, value-filled offer, they become skeptical and look for the catch.

I've personally experienced this in one of my businesses where we were offering a much better service at a price that was about half the price of our competitors. People kept ringing into the sales line to recap the offer that was on the website and to ask what the catch was.

I don't suggest you fabricate reasons for your offer but be ready to have a solid reason why you are offering a great deal, e.g. clearing old stock, damaged inventory, overstock, moving your office or warehouse, etc.

Value Stacking: Packing in many bonuses can make your offer seem like a no-brainer. This is a very smart move and can dramatically increase conversions. In fact I advocate where possible to make the bonuses more valuable than the main offer. Infomercials do this very well. "We'll double your offer," "That's not all..." etc.

Upsells: When your prospect is hot and in the buying frame of mind, this is the perfect time to offer them a complimentary product or service. This is where you have the perfect opportunity to tack on a high margin item even if the primary product you are selling is low margin. It's the fries with the burger, the extended warranty, the car rustproofing. It gives the customer added value and gives you more profit per transaction.

Payment Plan: This one is absolutely critical for high ticket items and can mean the difference between the customer balking and walking away or making the sale.

If something is $5,000, presenting it as 12 easy payments of $497 makes it a much easier pill to swallow. People generally think of their expenses on a monthly basis and $497 per month feels much easier than $5,000 in one lump sum.

Also notice that 12 x $497 adds up to more than $5,000. In fact it makes it almost $6,000. The first reason you want to do this is to cover your finance costs if you're financing the sale.

Second, you want to incentivize the people who can pay in a lump sum to receive a "discount" by paying upfront.

Guarantee: As discussed previously in this chapter, you need an outrageous guarantee. One that totally reverses the risk of doing business with you. People have been disappointed so many times that they don't trust any of the claims you make. It's nothing personal, just the way it is. You need to make dealing with you a risk-free transaction. In fact one where the risk is on you should you fail to deliver on your promises. "Satisfaction guaranteed" is weak and ineffective.

Scarcity: Your offer needs to have an element of scarcity. A reason why people need to respond immediately. People respond much more to a fear of loss than the prospect of gain. However, again you need a good "reason why" the scarcity exists as you don't want to be disingenuous with your scarcity claims.

You have a limited supply, limited time, limited resources. Use this to your advantage in your marketing. If you can have a running countdown of time or available stock this can further turn up the heat on the fear of loss emotion.

As you've seen there are many components to crafting a compelling offer. Taking the lazy, ill-thought-out road of "10% off" or similar crappy offers is akin to throwing your marketing dollars in the trash.

Take the time to craft a compelling, well-thought-out offer. Your conversion rate will skyrocket and so will your bottom line.

Target The Pain

You've got a splitting headache. You open your medicine cabinet and start rifling through your museum of half-used tablets, creams and vitamins only to realize you're totally out of pain relief medication. So you rush down to your local pharmacy in the hope of getting the tablet that's going to give you the relief you so desperately need.

Do you worry about the price? Does it even enter your mind to shop around and see if you can buy the same product cheaper at another pharmacy? Unlikely. You're in pain and you need immediate relief. In fact even if the tablets were priced at double or triple the normal price, you'd probably still buy.

The usual ways of shopping get thrown out the window when we're in pain. The exact same is true for your customers and prospects. So many times businesses talk about "features and benefits" rather than speaking to the pain that the customer already has. How much selling does a pharmacist need to do to sell pain relief medication to someone with a splitting headache? Very little I suspect.

The same is true whether you sell TVs, cars or consulting. You have prospects and customers who are in pain. They want pain relief, not features and benefits. If you're selling me a TV, you could sell me features and benefits by telling me it's got four HDMI ports and 1080p resolution. This will mean very little to most people. Imagine instead you target my pain point which is bringing it back home, unpacking it and spending an infuriating number of hours trying to get it working properly with all my other devices.

Instead of price discounting and positioning yourself as a commodity, why not offer to deliver it to my house, mount it on the wall, ensure the picture quality is spectacular and make sure that it works perfectly with all my other peripherals. Now you're giving me pain relief and price becomes less important than if you're selling me a commodity with a list of features and benefits.

In the above example, even though you might be selling the exact same TV as your competitor, if you package it up in a way that takes away my pain—then you've won my business. It's also much more likely I'll become a raving fan and refer others to you because you weren't just the vendor of a commodity. You were a problem solver. Now it's an apples-to-oranges comparison. How do you compare this to "it's got four HDMI ports and 1080p resolution"?

Selling features and benefits is the best way to turn your prospects into price shoppers who view your product as a commodity bought solely on price. Your goal is to be a problem solver, pain reliever and turn any comparison with your competition into an apples-to-oranges comparison. Remember people are much more willing to pay for a cure than for prevention. Targeting existing pain rather than promising future pleasure will result in much higher conversion, much higher customer satisfaction and lower price resistance. Look for pain points in your industry and become the source of relief.

Copywriting For Sales—You Can't Bore People Into Buying

Almost no other skill will reward you more richly than the ability to write compelling words. Being able to clearly articulate why a prospect should buy from you rather than your competitors in a way that creates an emotion and motivates them to action is the master skill of marketing.

Earlier in this book we touched on the fact that direct response marketing uses very different copywriting techniques. In direct response marketing we use copy which is designed to push the emotional hot buttons of the target audience.

Rather than using the conventional, boring, "professional" sounding copy, we use copy that is like a car accident—no matter how much you don't want to, you can't help but look.

Emotional direct response copywriting uses attention grabbing headlines, strong sales copy and compelling calls to action. It's what's known as "salesmanship in print."

Many businesses, especially those who sell products and services to professional or business customers feel like this type of copy is not appropriate for their market. And while it's true we should tailor our approach to this market (as we would for any target market), it would be a major mistake to discount emotional direct response copywriting.

From the CEO of a Fortune 500 company down to the janitor, we're all big bags of emotion and our buying decisions are made with emotion and then justified with logic later. "Hey honey, I bought that Porsche 911 because of safety and German cars are really reliable too." Yeah right.

So many times when I meet business owners in person I find their personality is completely different from the personality displayed in their marketing. Truth be told most display no personality in their marketing at all. The reason behind this is a perceived need to look "professional." Their marketing is often bland, generic and if you swapped out their logo and name from their marketing material, it could be anyone else in their industry. It's such a shame because if only they communicated in their marketing the way they do in person, they'd have much more success.

When you meet them in person, these people are often highly intelligent, interesting to listen to and passionate about what they do, yet when it comes to their marketing material and sales copy it's like they freeze up. All of a sudden, they try to sound "professional" and start using weasel words and phrases they would never normally use in conversation. You know the sort of words and phrases I mean, "best of breed products," "synergistic," "strategic alignment," etc. Words they'd never use in a real conversion with their friends or colleagues.

The fact is people buy from people, not from corporations. Building relationships and rapport is well understood in the world of one-to-one sales; however, for some reason when it comes to the one-to-many position of being a marketer, many business owners think they need to put their personality aside and behave like a faceless corporation. Copywriting is salesmanship in print. You need to write your sales copy as though you were talking directly to a single person.

Using monotone, boring, "professional" sales copy is the fastest way of losing the interest of your customers and prospects. Meaningless clichés and claims of being the leading provider in your category makes you look like a "me-too" business. "Me-too" businesses attract lowest common denominator clients who by necessity shop based on price as they have nothing else to differentiate you by.

People love authenticity, personality and opinion. Even if they don't agree with you, they'll respect you for being real and open. Being yourself and bringing out your personality will help you stand out in a sea of sameness and monotony. Just have a look at one of the most consistently enduring TV formats—the news talking head. Why waste such a large percentage of air time on showing the face of the presenter? Using just their voice-over would mean that a lot more content and visual footage of the news story could be broadcast.

However, the reason so much time is allocated to just the video of a talking head is that it adds personality to often bland topics. It also adds authority and feels like a one-on-one conversation with a trusted source.

People respond to pictures and videos of other people. It's no accident that YouTube and Facebook are two of the biggest online properties in the world. We're extremely interested in what other people are doing and saying.

You can easily take advantage of this in your business. One example is by adding a video to your website. It can be as simple as a talking head video of you describing your products and services, which you can shoot and upload in the space of five minutes using a handheld camera or even a smartphone. Another example is using social media as a two-way communication medium for engaging with customers and prospects. Doing just these two things will create deeper connections because you're adding personality to your business.

Don't use your marketing material as a screen to hide behind. Use it to give opinion, insight, advice and commentary and above all be yourself and be authentic. This will instantly create rapport and will differentiate you from all the other boring and bland marketing material around you.

People open their mail above a wastepaper basket and have their index finger hovering above the delete button when reading email. They sort it into two piles, the first pile gets opened and read and the second pile goes into the trash, often unopened. People are craving something new, something entertaining, something different. When you give that to them, you get their attention. When your copy is "professional," it's boring, monotone and ignored. The fact is that most businesses are too afraid to send out copy that will get them noticed. They fear what their friends, relatives, industry peers and others will think or say.

So they send out letters and ads which are timid and "me too." Swap the company name and logo and they are pretty much interchangeable with every one of their other competitors. There's really only one opinion you should be worrying about—that of your customers and prospects. Frankly no one else's opinion, including yours, should figure in what you put in your sales copy. Testing and measuring response is the only true way of judging the effectiveness of your copy.

The truth is the masses are living lives of quiet desperation. They are absolutely craving something that grabs or entertains them, even if it's just for a moment. Your job is to give it to them.

Elements Of Great Copy

It's incredible how a change in a word or phrase can dramatically change the effectiveness of an ad. The fact is there are some words which are extremely powerful and trigger emotional hot buttons. For example think about the following three words:

- Animal
- Fish
- Shark

Which of these three triggers the most emotional response in you? I suspect it's the last one, yet they could all be used to describe the same creature. The same is true of words you use when writing sales copy. Some words trigger a bigger emotional response than others. Here are just a small sample of the most common compelling words:

- Free
- You
- Save
- Results
- Health
- Love
- Proven
- Money
- New
- Easy
- Safety
- Guaranteed
- Discovery

A one word change in your headline can dramatically alter the results you achieve. Always remember, **people buy with emotions first and then justify with logic afterwards**. Trying to sell to their logical brain with facts and figures is a complete waste of time.

The five major motivators of human behavior, especially buying behavior are:

- Fear
- Love
- Greed
- Guilt
- Pride

If your sales copy isn't pushing at least one of these emotional hot buttons, then it's likely too timid and ineffective.

Headlines are one of the most important elements in your sales copy. Their job is to grab the attention of your target market and get them to start reading your body copy. The headline is basically the ad for the ad and should encompass the self-serving result your reader will get. You'll use headlines extensively in your marketing when writing email subject lines, sales letter headlines or web page titles. Here's a small sample of headlines from some of the most successful advertising campaigns throughout history:

- They Laughed When I Sat Down At The Piano—But When I Started To Play!
- Who Else Wants A Screen Star Figure?
- Amazing Secret Discovered By One-Legged Golfer Adds 50 Yards To Your Drives, Eliminates Hooks and Slices And Can Slash Up To 10 Strokes From Your Game Almost Overnight!
- Confessions Of A Disbarred Lawyer
- Have You Ever Seen A Grown Man Cry?
- An Open Letter To Every Overweight Person In Portland
- Is The Life Of A Child Worth $1 To You?
- How A Strange Accident Saved Me From Baldness
- When The Government Freezes Your Bank Account—What Then?
- How A "Fool Stunt" Made A Star Salesman
- Wife Of Famous Movie Star Swears Under Oath Her New Perfume Does Not Contain An Illegal Sexual Stimulant!

- Profits That Lie Hidden In Your Farm
- Proof: Doctors Are More Dangerous Than Guns!

Notice how all the successful, tested headlines above push one or more of the five major motivators of human behavior?

> **To get a list of hundreds of the most successful headlines in advertising history visit 1pmp.com**

Fear, especially the fear of loss is one of the most powerful emotional hot buttons you can push in your sales copy. Understanding how certain words link to certain emotions is powerful.

Many worry that this is too manipulative. Like any powerful tool it can be used for good or for evil purposes and no doubt many people do both.

A sharp knife in the hands of a surgeon can be used to save a life or in the hands of a criminal to take a life. Either way, we need to understand how this powerful tool works and likely we can't go through life avoiding its use.

The same thing is applied to emotional direct response copywriting. It's a powerful selling tool and you should never use it unethically.

If you sell something that is in the best interest of your prospect or customer then you are actually doing them a great service by using this powerful selling tool. You are preventing them from buying someone else's inferior product or service.

Enter The Conversation Already Going On In Your Prospect's Mind

We all have a conversation going on in our mind, all the time. Sometimes this is referred to as "inner talk."

That conversation is going to be very different if you are an expectant mother compared to a retiree. Or a fanatical fitness junkie compared to a couch potato. This is part of why it's so important to understand your target market well.

An emotional hot button for one type of target audience will fall on deaf ears to another audience. Emotional direct response copywriting is no substitute for understanding EXACTLY who your target audience is and what their emotional triggers are.

Before you ever write a single word of copy, you must intimately understand how your target market thinks and talks. The kind of language they use and respond to. What kind of day they have and the conversation that goes on in their mind. What are their fears and frustrations? What gets them excited and motivated?

Research is often the most neglected component of copywriting and is the major reason why even powerful copy can sometimes fail. Emotional direct response copywriting is a powerful tool in your marketing arsenal. But understand it is part of a process. Research, write, then test and measure and you'll be far ahead of 99.9% of all your competitors.

Another way to enter the conversation going on in your prospect's mind is to address the elephant in the room. It's natural to always try and present your business in the most favorable light possible when marketing yourself. However, this often leads to one of the most common marketing blunders—discussing only the positive aspects of doing business with you. Avoiding the elephant in the room, i.e. the risks associated with buying from you, is a rookie mistake.

The amygdala is the fear part of our brain. It governs our reactions to events that are important for our survival and it stimulates fear to warn us of imminent danger. If you're being followed at night by a suspicious looking individual and your heart is pounding, that's your amygdala doing its job. That's good. However, the amygdala in your prospect's brain can also stop them from buying from you. That's bad.

Whether you own a coffee shop or a hospital, when a prospective customer considers buying from you, their amygdala is making a judgment call about the potential risks involved. The risk being evaluated by the amygdala may be as trivial as a bad tasting latte or as severe as an untimely death on an operating table. Either way, the risk evaluation is always going on in the background. As a business owner and marketer you need to understand that. If you skirt around this issue in your marketing, you allow the amygdala in your prospect's brain to run wild and potentially kill the sale. Given that this risk evaluation will happen whether you like it or not, why not participate in it and give yourself the best chance of addressing any potential deal breakers before they get a chance to damage your bottom line?

Traditional selling tells us to overcome objections; however, in reality, objections are rarely voiced. Instead in our polite society we say nonsense things like, "let me think about it" while inside the amygdala is screaming "let's get out of here." Part of the job of good sales copy is to tell potential prospects who your product or service is NOT for. There are three very good reasons you should do this.

First, it filters out people who aren't part of your target market or those who wouldn't be a good fit for what you have to offer. This ensures you don't waste your time on low quality, low probability prospects. It also reduces the number of refunds and complaints from customers who misunderstood what they bought.

Second, it immediately makes it more credible when you tell them who this product is for. It feels much more even handed when you cover both angles by telling them who it is for and who it isn't for.

Last, the prospects who it is for will feel the product or service is much more tailored to their needs versus if you had said your product is for anyone and everyone. It feels more targeted and exclusive.

Another excellent way to enter the mind of your prospect is to find out what they blame and use a device in your copy known as "the enemy in common." If you ask most people why they haven't achieved success, some of the most common responses include:

- The economy
- The government
- Taxes are too high
- Poor upbringing or parenting
- Unsupportive family or friends
- No time
- No money
- No opportunity
- Lack of skills or education
- Unfair boss

There's just one thing wrong with this list—they aren't on it!

Here are the results of a national survey which was conducted by one of the major newspapers on "cost of living pressure" also known as spending too much and earning too little. You can see how few people blame themselves for their current circumstances.

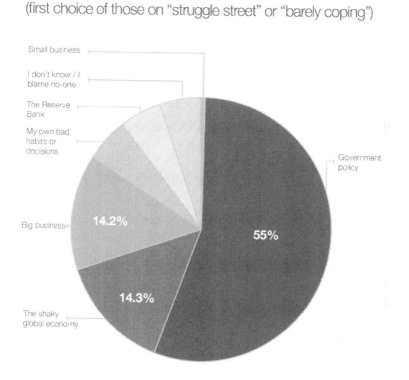

Who do you blame for cost of living pressure?
(first choice of those on "struggle street" or "barely coping")

According to the *Journal of Safety Research*[5], 74% of Americans believe they are above average drivers. Yet only 1% believe they are below average.

It's the same with accepting blame. How many times have you heard a child say "It's Not My Fault"? As adults, people are much the same. Most of us don't believe we are in the wrong. So what can you do with this knowledge? First, in your sales copy never blame your prospects for the position they are in. If we're going to enter the conversation

---

[5]   Journal of Safety Research Vol 34, 2003

already going on in their mind, our marketing message needs to take into account these existing thought processes—no matter how foreign they are from our own.

"The enemy in common" is a great way of leveraging the "it's not my fault" mentality. Take something relevant from your prospect's blame list, side with them and tie it into a solution you have to offer. Here's a sample headline that an accountant could use:

> "Free Report Reveals How To Reclaim Your Hard Earned Cash From The Greedy Tax Man"

This is a great way of bonding with your prospect while offering them a solution. By using a common enemy, you connect with the prospect, and you're seen as the savior against a foe—in this case, government taxes.

"The enemy in common" rattles their cage, enters the conversation already going on in their mind and stirs up the emotions that are already there just below the surface.

It's a great way to break through the clutter and get your prospect's attention.

How To Name Your Product, Service Or Business

I've had "the naming discussion" with entrepreneurs many times. It usually goes like this—I'll be asked for my opinion on a new name or several variations thereof for a new product, service or business venture. Then often follows an explanation of the name or names which are being considered. Here's my take on naming—if you need to explain the name, to me that's an automatic fail. Title should equal content. In other words if the name doesn't make it automatically obvious what the product, service or business is, then you're starting from behind. When I give people this advice some shake their heads in disbelief. What about great brands with unusual names like Nike, Apple, Skype, Amazon, etc.? Surely I must be missing something by giving such simplistic advice? Here's the thing. All of the big brands spend hundreds of millions of dollars in advertising to educate people about who they are and what they do. How much are you willing to spend to do the same?

Here we're not even talking about advertising that sells or generates leads. We're talking about advertising that merely tells people what you do. I can't think of a bigger waste of money. By using a non-obvious name, you're starting from behind and then have to make up for by spending a lot of money on advertising to rectify the situation. All you had to do to avoid this colossal waste of money was call your business "Fast Plumbing Repairs," which immediately explains what you do and what you stand for, rather than "Aqua Solutions" after which you have to explain that Aqua is the Latin for water and that you provide "complete plumbing solutions" (whatever that means) hence the name "Aqua Solutions."

So many times I've seen a business or product name whose meaning is unclear. Sometimes it's a corny play on words, other times it's an obscure literary reference and still other times it's some made up word, the meaning of which is only apparent to the creator. The reality is no matter how clever your name is, very few people will go to the trouble of trying to decipher its meaning or origin. These things may be important to you because it's your baby, but rarely does a customer or prospect give it even a split second of thought.

What's even worse is that being "clever" often creates confusion and works against you. As we covered earlier in this chapter confusion leads to lost sales. If you confuse them, you lose them. It's that simple. **Always choose clarity over cleverness**. It's hard enough to get a message read, understood then acted upon at the best of times. But intentionally adding confusion into the mix when you're a small business with a modest marketing budget is madness.

Lastly, please don't ask friends and family for their opinion on your clever new name. They'll of course praise your idea and compliment you, which feels nice, but it's unlikely to be truly helpful. By all means test and get opinions but do so from objective people who are part of your target market—not from those who already know what you're about. Naming can work for you or against you and it's expensive and difficult to change down the track, so give it thought, effort and above all else focus on clarity.

Chapter 2 Action Item:
What Is Your Message To Your Target Market?
Fill in square #2 of your 1-Page Marketing Plan

Chapter 3

Reaching Prospects
With Advertising Media

Chapter 3 Summary

Advertising media is the vehicle you'll use to reach your target market and communicate your message. It's typically the most expensive component of your marketing, so it needs to be selected and managed carefully to ensure you get a good return on investment (ROI).

Highlights covered in this chapter include:

- How to measure the effectiveness of a marketing campaign.
- Why "getting your name out there" is a losing strategy.
- How to get a good return on investment (ROI) when advertising.
- The lifetime value of a customer and how this is split up between the "front end" and "back end."
- The role that social media plays in your business.
- How to effectively use email and postal mail as part of your media strategy.
- How to protect your business from "a single point of failure."

The ROI Game

John Wanamaker, one of the marketing greats, famously said:

"Half the money I spend on advertising is wasted; the trouble is I don't know which half"

While this was understandable a century ago, when it was first said, it should be a crime to say that today. Yet the reality is that most small businesses do little if any tracking of advertising. Not measuring where your leads and sales come from and not tracking ROI on ad spend is the mark of the amateur. We all have at our disposal the technology to quickly, easily and cheaply track advertising effectiveness.

Tools such as toll-free numbers, website analytics and coupon codes make this trivial. Remember **what gets measured, gets managed**. Be ruthless with your ad spend by cutting the losers and riding the winners. Obviously to know what's losing and what's winning, you need to be tracking and measuring.

This is vital because media is by far the most expensive component of your marketing spend. It's the bridge that connects your offer to your target market. Whether you're using traditional media like radio, TV and print or newer digital media like social, search engine optimization (SEO) and email marketing, you need to understand the idiosyncrasies of each.

It's well beyond the scope of this book to go into the technical details of each category and subcategory of media. However, I'd give you this piece of general advice: hire experts that specialize in whatever media you decide is right for your campaign—they're worth their weight in gold. Don't try and do it yourself, especially when it comes to the most expensive part of your marketing process. **What you don't know WILL hurt you**. Whether you're using online media like social, email or web, or offline media like direct mail, print or radio, each has its own idiosyncrasies and technicalities that you're highly likely to mess up if you're not experienced with it. It would be a tragedy to get the target market and offer right and then have your campaign flop because you messed up a technical detail in your media.

I'm often asked questions like, "What's a good response rate for direct mail?" or "What kind of open rate should I expect when doing email marketing?" The expectation is that I'll give a numerical answer. Something like, "Expect a 2% response rate from direct mail" or "Expect a 20% open rate for email."

Usually these kinds of questions come from well-meaning business owners who are yet to build their marketing infrastructure. My answer is always the same—it depends. Sometimes a 50% response rate is a disaster and sometimes a 0.01% response rate is a massive success.

Response rates will vary dramatically depending on factors such as how relevant the message is to the target market, how compelling the offer is and how you came about the list you're marketing to. Instead of asking what a good response rate is, which is a nonsense question, they're really asking, "How do I measure the success of my marketing campaign?"

So how do you measure the success of a marketing campaign?

For the impatient, here's the short answer: did the marketing campaign make you more money than it cost you? Another way of putting it is, what was the return on investment (ROI) on the marketing campaign? If it cost you more than you made (or will ever make) on this campaign then it's a failure. If it cost you less than the profits you made as result of the campaign then it's a success.

Of course some people will argue with me and say that even a campaign that lost money was valuable because it "got your name out there" or was some sort of "branding" exercise. Unless you're a mega brand like Nike, Apple, Coca-Cola or similar then it's likely you can't afford to burn tens of millions of dollars on fuzzy marketing like "branding" or "getting your name out there."

Rather than "getting your name out there," you'll fare much better by concentrating on getting the name of your prospects in here.

I like to think of marketing dollars as firepower. You need to use your limited firepower wisely so that you can successfully hunt, come home victorious and feed your family. However, if you start randomly firing in every direction, you're going to startle and scare off your prey. You need to be targeted and clever if you wish to be victorious.

If you're a small or medium sized business you need to get a return on your marketing spend. Putting your comparatively tiny marketing budget into fuzzy marketing would have the same effect as a kid peeing in the ocean.

The game of mass marketing/branding/getting your name out there type of marketing can only be won with atomic bomb scale firepower. If you're a small to medium business, that's not a game you're equipped to play. That being the case we need to look at the numbers carefully.

Let's run through an example with some numbers to illustrate. I'll keep the numbers small and round for the sake of clarity.

You do a direct mail campaign and send out one hundred letters.

The cost of printing and mailing the one hundred letters is $300.

Out of one hundred letters, ten people respond (10% response rate).

Out of the ten people who responded, two people end up buying from you (20% closure rate).

From this we can work out one of the most important numbers in marketing—customer acquisition cost. In this example, you acquired two customers and the campaign cost you a total of $300. So your customer acquisition cost is $150.

Now if the product or service you sell these customers makes you a profit of only $100 per sale, then this was a losing campaign. You lost $50 for every customer acquired in this campaign (negative ROI).

However, let's say the product or service you sell makes you a profit of $600 per sale, then this is a winning campaign. You made $450 for every customer acquired (positive ROI).

Now obviously this is a simplistic example but it illustrates how irrelevant statistics like response rates and conversion rates are. Our primary concern is return on investment, which varies based on the customer acquisition cost and how much actual profit a marketing campaign yields.

One of the massive advantages of targeting a niche is that your marketing becomes much cheaper. Targeted advertising ends up being much cheaper than mass marketing because there is far less waste.

If you're selling photography of newborn babies you'd be far better served advertising in "New Mother Magazine" than putting a general photography ad in the classifieds.

Your customer acquisition cost will drop dramatically because your message to market match is much better and hence your conversion rate will be much higher than if you had a general message in your ad.

Your advertising costs would also be lower because your target market is smaller.

Remember the entire goal of your ad is for your prospect to say, "Hey that's for me."

Being all things to all people is unlikely to have the same reaction.

The "Front End," "Back End" and Lifetime Value Of A Customer

With the above example we determined that if we made only $100 of profit per sale then we had a losing campaign. However, in that example we didn't take into account one of the other very important numbers used in measuring marketing success, **customer lifetime value**.

If for example we make $100 directly as a result of the campaign but then the customer continues to buy from us down the track, that completely changes the economics of the campaign. A campaign that looked like a loser can in fact become a winner when we take into account their lifetime value as a customer.

We now need to take into account how much we'll likely make on a customer over their entire tenure with us. For example you might sell printers that require refills or a car that requires servicing or some other service that a customer buys repeatedly, e.g. haircuts, massage, insurance, Internet access, etc.

The money we make upfront on a campaign is known as "the front end." The money we make on subsequent purchases is known as "the back end." Together these figures make up the lifetime value of a customer.

Lifetime value and customer acquisition cost are two of the key numbers you need to know to measure marketing effectiveness. The other statistics like response rates and conversion rates in themselves are useless. We just use them to determine these two figures, which give us a true picture of how our marketing is performing.

If you don't know what these numbers are in your business, then now's the time to start measuring and making your marketing accountable. Constantly testing, measuring and improving these numbers is how you build a high growth business.

Your "front end" offer is the offer that gets seen by prospects (people who aren't yet your customers). These are people who don't know you and have no reason to like you or trust you. In general, the goal of your front end offer is to create a customer and make enough profit from the first transaction to at least cover the customer acquisition cost. This makes it very sustainable to keep advertising. The real profit is made on the "back end" through repeat purchases by existing customers.

Sometimes it makes sense to "go negative," that is lose money on the front end because you know for certain you'll make it up and more on the back end. This is often the case with subscription businesses or businesses that have a high lifetime value. If you don't know your numbers, this can be a risky strategy, so stick to the goal having your front end pay for your customer acquisition cost until you have a good handle on your lifetime value numbers. In Chapter 8 we'll talk more about the back end and increasing customer lifetime value. This can revolutionize your business and turn losing campaigns into winners.

Is Social Media A Cure All?

Without a doubt the Internet and social media are media breakthroughs. They've democratized information and have made possible a level of connectedness never before possible. However, there's also a lot of hype that surrounds these forms of "new media," as they're often referred to. Especially with all the hype that surrounds social media, you'd imagine it was a marketing cure all. Many self-proclaimed social media "gurus" would have you believe that social media is the future of all marketing and that if you're not dedicating all or most of your marketing resources to social media, you're a luddite who'll soon be out of business.

Of course as with most hype, there's a need to keep a level head in order to separate fact from fiction. Before I'm labeled as being against social media, let me set the record straight. I've used social media in multiple businesses and continue to use it on a regular basis.

However, because there's so much hype that surrounds social media, I want to put it in perspective for you and help you see where it fits into an overall marketing strategy.

A successful marketing campaign has to get three vital elements right:

Market (covered in Chapter 1) – The target market you send your message to

Message (covered in Chapter 2) – The marketing message or offer you send

Media (covered in this chapter) – The vehicle that you use to communicate your message to your target market, e.g. radio, direct mail, telemarketing, Internet, TV, etc.

You need to hit all three of these to have a successful campaign. You need to send the right message to the right target market, through the right media channel. Failing at any one of these three elements will likely cause your marketing campaign to fail. Understanding this framework helps put things in context. Social media, by definition is a **media**—it's not a strategy.

The time-tested fundamentals of marketing don't suddenly change just because a new type of media comes along. The next thing to ask—is it the right media for your business? Remember of the three things we need to get right for a successful campaign, media is one of them. Every type of media has its idiosyncrasies and social media is no exception. Here are some of the things you need to be aware of when it comes to social media.

First, it's not the ideal selling environment. I like to think of social media as a social gathering or party. We've all been to gatherings where someone, perhaps a family member or friend has been bitten by the multi-level marketing bug. You know where they start spruiking the health benefits of the latest pills or potions and try to sell or recruit others to sell.

It makes everyone uncomfortable because it feels pushy and feels like an inappropriate time to be making or receiving a sales pitch. Social media is exactly the same. Overt selling and constant pitching of offers is generally considered poor behavior on social networks and can result in repelling people from your business rather than attracting them.

However, just like a real life social gathering, social media is a great place to create and extend relationships which can later turn into something commercial if there's a good fit. One of the most valuable things I see in social media is being able to gauge customer emotions toward your business and engage with vocal customers who offer either praise or complaints in a public forum.

A side benefit of this is social proof. Being accessible, responding to criticism or praise and engaging with your customers builds social proof and makes prospects and customers feel like they are dealing with humans rather than a faceless corporation. Remember people buy from people.

There are two potential traps with social media.

First, it can be a time suck. Feeling like you have to respond to every inane comment can be draining and it can suck time away from marketing tasks that can give you a far better return on time and money invested. It's important to be disciplined with your use of social media. Just like you wouldn't let your employees stand around and chit chat all day, you can't let yourself or them get carried away with the online equivalent. Some people have the perception that social media marketing is "free". It's only truly if your time is worth nothing.

Second, there's the question of ownership. Your social media page and profile is actually the property of the social network. So spending huge amounts of time and money building up a profile and audience on these networks ends up building up their assets rather than your own.

My preference as much as possible is to build and own my own marketing assets such as websites, blogs, email lists, etc. I then use social media simply as a way to drive traffic to these marketing assets. This way, my time and effort goes into renovating my own "house" rather than that of a landlord who can kick me out at any time.

A classic example of why you want to do this is Facebook's change of policy on business pages. Previously if people "Liked" your business's

Facebook page you could freely reach this entire audience for free. So businesses spent a lot of time, money and effort getting people to "Like" them on their Facebook page.

Now Facebook requires you to pay them each time you want to send a message to your entire audience, otherwise it only allows you to reach a small percentage. For those who spent huge resources on building up a Facebook audience only to have the rug pulled out from under them, this came as a huge blow.

This is one of the reasons why personally I'd prefer to have 1,000 people on my own email list than 10,000 people who "Like" my Facebook page.

As always with any marketing strategy it's vitally important to find out where your prospects "hang out" and use the appropriate media to get your message through to them. Social media may or may not be one of those places they hang out.

Email Marketing

Email is a direct, personal way to engage with prospects and customers. Thanks to the proliferation of smartphones and mobile devices, pretty much everyone has email in their pocket or within easy reach.

Building a database of email subscribers plays a central role in your online marketing strategy. A prominent part of your website should be an email opt-in form. This enables you to capture the email address of website visitors and gives you the opportunity to nurture those visitors who may not be ready to buy immediately but who are interested and want more information.

As we'll discuss in the next two chapters, lead capture and lead nurturing are two critical stages of the marketing process. They give us the ability to intelligently deal with interested prospects that may not yet be developed to the point of making a purchasing decision. Generally, these kinds of prospects make up the majority of all prospects and are crucial to filling your pipeline of future sales. If you didn't capture these interested non-buyers you'd likely lose them forever. Your only hope would be that when they finally became ready to buy, they would remember your website among hundreds they may have visited and complete the buying cycle they began days, weeks or months ago.

Email also enables you to maintain a close relationship with your customer base and makes it easy to test and launch new products and services. Over time as you build a relationship with your email subscribers, your database becomes an increasingly valuable marketing asset.

Having a highly responsive list of email subscribers enables you to almost create cash on demand. You create a compelling offer with a response mechanism and send an email blast to your list. You'll get instant feedback whether it's a hit or a miss. It's a great way of cheaply testing offers prior to investing in more expensive media such as print or pay-per-click advertising.

Despite the growth and popularity of social media, your database of email subscribers remains one of the most important elements of your online marketing strategy. As discussed in the previous few pages, social media reach has become problematic because only a small percentage of your followers will actually see your message. Even if your message were allowed to reach everyone, you'd probably get drowned out in all the noise. Funny cat videos, jokes and memes will crowd out your marketing message. It's called **social** media for a reason.

Even more importantly an email database is an asset that **you** own. It's independent of whatever social media property may be the flavor of the month. Remember MySpace? While I don't think Facebook or Twitter are going away soon, it is a fast moving space. If you build your business on someone else's platform and it starts to decline in popularity, your key online marketing asset becomes stranded.

While email is a powerful media, it does have a few idiosyncrasies that you must be aware of. Here are some of the key dos and don'ts when it comes to email.

Don't spam. There are strict rules about email marketing in most countries. Most notably that you must have the consent of the email recipient to send them marketing emails. That's why an opt-in form on your website is critical. Never ever buy or compile lists of email addresses where the recipients haven't explicitly requested to be emailed. Not only is this very poor positioning, putting you in the same category as spammers, but it's also illegal. We'll discuss positioning in much more detail in Chapter 6.

Be human. Don't write an email like a robot or like you're writing a formal letter. Email is a very personal media and even if you're sending the same email to thousands of subscribers, write as though you're emailing a single person. Feel free to be a bit informal.

Use a commercial email marketing system. Don't ever use Outlook, Gmail or any other standard email service for mass email marketing. These services are designed for one-to-one emails not one-to-many. Your account will either get shut down or blacklisted if you start mass emailing from these services. There are commercial email marketing systems that are cheap and easy to use. Some popular ones are AWeber, MailChimp, Infusionsoft, and ActiveCampaign. The great thing about using these services is that they automatically take care of a lot of the legal compliance for you, things like having an unsubscribe option and your contact details at the bottom of your marketing emails. They also work hard to bypass spam filters and ensure good deliverability.

Email regularly. If you rarely email your email database they'll start to go "cold." They may have opted into your email database but if they haven't heard from you for a long time, they may forget who you are and mark you as a spammer. Worse still, the value of your key online marketing asset starts to decay. To keep the relationship warm, stay in touch with your email subscribers at the very least monthly. Best practice is closer to weekly but it also depends on your target market. I know some email marketers who email daily or even multiple times a day. There are no hard and fast rules when it comes to frequency. Just ensure when you email it's relevant and value building.

Give them value. If you only ever email your subscriber database when you want to sell them something, this will quickly get old and they'll either unsubscribe from your list, ignore your emails or mark you as a spammer. All healthy relationships are based on an exchange of value. Ensure the majority of your emails are not sales pitches but rather something that creates value for your subscribers. A good ratio is three value building emails for every offer email.

Automate. Another great reason to use a commercial email marketing platform is automation. These platforms allow you to set up sequences that automatically get emailed to new subscribers. For example when they subscribe, you could have your email marketing platform automatically send them a welcome email. A day later it could send them a value-packed email helping them to better understand the product category they're interested in. Three days later it could send an email telling them more about you and your business. A week later it could invite them to schedule a phone call with you. All this can be done on autopilot. An email marketing platform can be one of the best salespeople in your organization. It will never take a sick day, never complain and never forget to follow up.

With email marketing you have three challenges:

- **Getting your email delivered**. As discussed, the best way to ensure good email deliverability is to use a commercial email marketing platform. In addition to that, ensure that your email copy doesn't contain spammy phrases or use too many images or links.
- **Getting your email opened**. The best way to get your email opened is to have a compelling subject line. In the copywriting section of Chapter 2 we discussed copywriting strategy and headlines. Imagine your email among hundreds of others in your prospect's inbox. The job of your email subject line is to create curiosity and motivate the recipient to open your email.
- **Getting your email read**. Some marketers advocate that you should keep emails to subscribers short. In reality, the length of your emails is secondary to their relevance and quality. If you write compelling content it will get read. For example prominent email marketer and blogger Ramit Sethi writes very long emails. He also emails his subscribers frequently. He has collected thousands of data points on his target market and knows exactly what they want to read. So while his emails are long, they are highly relevant and compelling to his target market. An alternative approach is to keep emails short by only having a teaser or summary in the email body. Readers are then invited to click on a link so they can read more on your website or blog.

Email is a very powerful and personal media channel. It allows you to create compelling campaigns with a high degree of automation. When done right it can be a valuable part of both an online and offline media strategy.

Snail Mail

In an age where the Internet, email and social media play such huge roles in our personal and business communications, many have taken the view that postal mail or "snail mail" is all but dead. Nothing could be further from the truth.

I'm extremely tech savvy and I've grown up with the Internet from its early dial-up days and prior. I've also been a co-founder of two very successful tech startups that I helped build from zero right through to rapid growth and exit. Yet despite this background, or perhaps because of it, I regard "snail mail" as one of the most important and underutilized forms of media for marketing. When it comes to your media strategy you should understand that **email doesn't replace postal mail, it complements it.**

We all love the speed and efficiency of all things virtual; however, it would be a mistake to underestimate the power of physical objects when it comes to moving people emotionally. And **moving people emotionally towards a desired action is what marketing is all about.** Imagine a man sending his wife an "I love you" text or email on their anniversary versus the same message communicated with a handwritten card with a bunch of her favorite flowers. There's a world of difference between the virtual and physical equivalents of the same message.

Have you ever received one of those Google AdWords coupon postcards in the mail? It's instructive that the poster child for the digital age, Google, uses postal mail as part of its small business marketing strategy. Postal mail has a much longer lifespan and requires effort to dispose of. It's not uncommon for people to treasure and keep postal letters from significant people in their lives for decades. The same would rarely be the case for emails which are ephemeral—in your inbox one moment, deleted and forgotten about the next.

Another important point about postal mail is that it has gotten significantly less cluttered over the past few years, which from a marketer's perspective is a dream come true. Clutter is the enemy of message cut through and having a media that has actually become less cluttered makes it all the more compelling. Conversely, email has become orders of magnitude more cluttered. The noise within email inboxes has gotten to ridiculous proportions and even someone who is good at sorting it approaches it with a completely different frame of mind to postal mail. People handle their email with a finger hovering over the delete key. Anything that isn't immediately actionable gets deleted, forwarded or forgotten about in an inbox archive.

Until we figure out how to teleport physical objects from one location to another, like they do on Star Trek, we're reliant on couriers and the postal service to transport postal mail and physical objects for us.

Without doubt, postal mail is a powerful media channel. However, as with all media it's important not to get hung up or tied to a single channel. Your goal is to figure out how to get a good return on your media investment whether that be postal mail or anything else.

How To Have An Unlimited Marketing Budget

No discussion of marketing or spending on media can be complete without discussing budget. When spending money on marketing one of the following three things will occur:

1. Your marketing fails (i.e. you make less in profit than you spent on your marketing expenses).
2. You have no idea if your marketing was a success or failure because you don't measure the results.
3. Your marketing succeeds (i.e. you make more in profit than you spent on your marketing).

For each of these scenarios there's a simple course of action:

If your marketing consistently fails and loses you money then STOP and change what you're doing.

If you don't measure your marketing results that's just plain stupid because with the technology we have readily and cheaply available, it's easier than ever to track your marketing results and return on investment (ROI).

If your marketing is working and consistently giving you a positive ROI, then you should crank it up and throw as much money as you can at it.

One of the craziest things I see small business owners doing is setting a "marketing budget." By setting a marketing budget you are implying that either your marketing isn't working and hence it's a pure expense (i.e. a waste of money). Or you have no idea if it's working because you don't measure the results and so you throw money at it in the hope that it's giving you some sort of positive result. If it's the former then of course you need to set a budget because you can't have expenses running wild in your business. But a good question might be—why are you wasting money on marketing that isn't working? If it's the latter then you need to change things pronto. You wouldn't hire an employee and not measure their productivity, so why on earth would you consistently pay for marketing and not know what result it's generating?

If your marketing is working (i.e. giving you a positive return on investment) why on earth would you limit it with a budget? It's like having a legal money printing press. This scenario is called money at a discount. If I was selling $100 bills for $80, wouldn't you buy as many as you could possibly get your hands on? Or would you say, "sorry my budget for discounted $100 bills this month is only $800, I'll just take ten please."

That's why I always say have an unlimited budget for marketing that works. One argument I hear against this is concern about being able to handle the demand. Firstly, that's a great problem to have. Secondly, if you're truly receiving more demand than you can fill, this is the perfect opportunity to raise your prices. This will instantly boost your margins and bring you a better quality of client.

The only time to set a marketing budget is when you're in the testing phase. In the testing phase I advocate that you fail often and fail cheap until you have a winner. Test your headline, your offer, your ad positioning and other variables. Then cut the losers and optimize the winners until you finally have a combination that gives you the best possible return on investment.

Remember the post office charges you the same amount to mail a crappy direct mail piece that bombs as they do a high-converting direct mail piece that pulls in millions. Once you have a winner that pulls in more than it costs you, crank up the marketing spend and hence the speed of your legal money printing press!

The Most Dangerous Number

One is the most dangerous number in your business. It makes businesses brittle.

Does your business have only one source of leads? One major supplier? One major customer? Rely on one type of media? Offer one type of product? To borrow a computer system term, does your business have "a single point of failure?" If so your business is brittle and a small change in circumstances outside of your control could have a devastating effect.

That's a very tough situation to end up in. Many businesses were hit hard when Google changed its search engine algorithm. These businesses put all their marketing budget and effort on search engine optimization and literally overnight found themselves with no other source of leads.

Similarly when Google started to make changes to the types of paid ads it wanted to show, even advertisers who were paying Google enormous amounts of money each month, were hit with the "Google Slap." That is Google started to charge them four, five, sometimes even ten times as much as they did previously. This change forced the advertiser to stop their campaigns and try to fix the issue or find another source of leads. In the meantime, their business virtually stopped. Fax broadcasting was effectively outlawed in the United States and many businesses that relied on that as a sole source of leads went broke.

Some wise words of antiquity recommend that we build our house on a rock mass instead of on sand. That way when the storm inevitably comes, our house doesn't cave in. The first step is to identify any scenarios where the number one can potentially hurt you. Here are some examples:

- What if your largest customer leaves you for a competitor or what if they go out of business?
- What if there is a change of government legislation and the product you currently offer gets outlawed or regulated into oblivion?
- What if your main advertising strategy stops working?
- What if your advertising costs rise dramatically?
- What if your currently high search engine rankings disappear or pay-per-click rates rise sharply?
- What if your biggest supplier raises prices, has a supply shortage or goes out of business?
- What if you rely on email marketing and the government cracks down further on this strategy?

All of these scenarios can and do happen. If you rely on one of anything, you are leaving yourself in an exposed position—you're effectively building your house on a sandy foundation. When the storm comes and the floods rise, the house is going to collapse. Identify and eliminate single points of failure in your business.

That way, if the laws change, if the advertising rates go up, if all of a sudden one specific strategy stops working as well as it used to, your business will be safe. You'll be the one with the power because you are not reliant on one of anything. Jim Rohn had an excellent philosophy on the matter:

> *"You've got to think winter in the summer. It's just too easy to get faked out when the sky is blue and the clouds are fleecy. You've got to prepare for winter because it's coming, it always does."*

In the meantime even if none of these scenarios come to pass, at least you'll have built a more resilient and valuable business.

A common scenario I see when it comes to media strategy is that many small businesses have only one source of new business. I advocate having at least five different sources of new leads and new customers. Further I recommend that most of these five sources be in paid media, i.e. they cost you money to market yourself. The reason paid media is so important is twofold.

First, it's extremely reliable. If I pay a newspaper to run my ad, there's an extremely high probability the ad will actually be run. It's much harder to get such reliable and consistent lead flow from free (or seemingly free) marketing methods such as word of mouth.

Second, paid marketing forces you to focus on return on investment (ROI). If a paid marketing method is not working, you cut it. You don't waste further time or money on it. Whereas when the marketing method is nominally free, such as with word of mouth, we tend to be less ruthless and often end up wasting huge amounts of time because we didn't have to pay anything upfront. However, there's an opportunity cost which, if careful analysis is done, often translates to a surprisingly large amount of real money.

The art and science of being able to consistently turn a dollar of paid advertising into a dollar or more in profits through direct response marketing will make your business resilient and can help you turn the tap on to rapid business growth.

Chapter 3 Action Item:
What Media Will You Use To Reach Your Target Market?
Fill in square #3 of your 1-Page Marketing Plan

ACT II

The "During" Phase

The "During" Phase Section Summary

In the "during" phase you're dealing with leads. Leads are people that know you and have indicated interest in what you have to offer by responding to your marketing message. In this phase you'll capture these interested leads in a database system, nurture them with regular value-building information and convert them into paying customers.

The goal of this phase is to get your leads to like you and what you have to offer enough to buy from you for the first time. Once they've bought from you, they become a customer and enter the third and final phase of your marketing process.

Chapter 4

Capturing Leads

Chapter 4 Summary

Capturing leads in a database system for future follow-up is critical to your marketing success.

This is because only a very small percentage of interested leads may be ready to purchase from you immediately. Lead capture is all about properly handling interest and building your future sales pipeline.

Highlights covered in this chapter include:

- Why you should never try to sell directly from an advertisement and what to do instead.
- How to transition from "hunting" to "farming" and ensure you always have a full pipeline of new business.
- Why you shouldn't treat all prospects equally.
- How to use an "ethical bribe" to uncover high probability prospects.
- How to instantly increase the effectiveness of your advertising by 1,233%.
- Why some businesses get a constant flow of leads and prospects while others struggle.
- How to be seen as an expert and authority by your target market.

Hunting vs. Farming

Imagine yourself as a hunter. You wake up in the morning, gather your weapons and head out to the hunt. Some days you come back with a kill and your family eats a feast. Other days you come back empty handed and your family goes hungry. The pressure is on every single day to hunt successfully—it's a constant battle.

Now imagine yourself as a farmer. You plant your seeds and wait for them to be ready for the harvest. In the meantime, you nurture them and treat them with care. You water and tend to your crop. When they're ready, you start harvesting. In my experience, most businesses are hunters—not farmers:

- They cold call to generate new business
- They spend huge amounts of time and energy trying to get a new customer and do anything to close the sale as soon as possible
- Their advertising reeks of desperation as they try discounting and competing on price just to make a quick sale
- They waste huge amounts of time pestering people who are not interested in their product or service

Most business owners are clueless about the purpose behind their marketing. They slap the name of their business on their ad with a pretty logo and some meaningless slogan claiming to be the leader in their industry or area. If you ask them what the purpose of their advertising is, most will say it's to sell their products or to "get their name out there." This is **wrong**! Dead wrong. They may as well be flushing money down the toilet.

In direct response marketing, the purpose of your advertising is to find people who are interested in what you do, rather than trying to make an immediate sale from the ad. When you interested leads respond, you put them on your follow-up database so that you can build value for them, position yourself as an authority and create a relationship built on trust.

After doing this, the sale comes (if it's right for them) as a natural consequence. This will take a mindset shift but is an absolutely vital concept to understand.

Why not try to sell to them from your ad? It's true that some people reading your ad might be ready to buy immediately, but **the vast majority** will not be ready to make a purchasing decision on the very day they read your ad—even if they are interested in what you do.

If you don't put them in a database then you've lost them. They might have been ready to buy in a month, six months or a year. But since your advertising was "one-shot" you've completely wasted that opportunity. Your chances of them remembering your one-shot ad from six months ago is extremely slim.

This kind of marketing is similar to farming. It is an investment in your future because as your database grows, so will your business and your results.

Mining For Gold With The Ethical Bribe

Even in a narrow target market, all prospects should not be treated equally.

All other things being equal, the more money you can spend marketing to high probability prospects, the better your chances are of converting them to a customer.

Just like the proverbial archer mentioned in Chapter 1, who has a limited number of arrows, you have a limited supply of money for your marketing campaign, so it's essential you invest it wisely.

For example if you have $1,000 to spend on an ad campaign which reaches 1,000 people, you're essentially spending $1 per prospect.

Now assume that out of the 1,000 people the ad reaches, 100 are potential prospects for your product. By treating them equally, as you would have to do with mass marketing, you're wasting $900 on uninterested and unmotivated prospects to reach the 100 who are interested.

What if instead of treating them all equally you could sift, sort and screen so that you were only dealing with high probability prospects and not wasting valuable time and marketing dollars on uninterested and unmotivated prospects?

You could then spend the whole $1,000 on the 100 high probability prospects. That would allow you to spend $10 on wooing each of them instead of the measly $1 per prospect you'd have if you treated them all equally.

With ten times the firepower aimed at the right targets, do you think we'd have a better conversion rate? Of course.

But how do we separate the wheat from the chaff? The short answer is we bribe them into telling us!

Don't worry, there's nothing underhanded here. We offer an "ethical bribe" to get them to identify themselves to us. For example, our friend the photographer could offer a free DVD telling prospective brides exactly what they should look for in a wedding photographer and showcasing some of his work.

A very simple lead generating ad could be headlined: "Free DVD Reveals The Seven Costly Mistakes To Avoid When Choosing A Photographer For Your Wedding Day."

Anyone requesting this "ethical bribe" would be identifying themselves as a high probability prospect. You now have at least their name and address which would go onto your marketing database.

Remember the goal is simply to generate leads. Avoid the temptation of trying to sell from your ad. At this early stage you just want to sift out the uninterested and unmotivated so that you can build your database of high probability prospects.

Here's the other big reason you want to avoid selling directly from your ad: at any given time (on average) about 3% of your target market are highly motivated and ready to buy immediately. These are the prospects most mass marketing hopes to convert. However, there's a further 7% who are very open to buying and another 30% who are interested but not right now. The next 30% are not interested and finally the last 30% wouldn't even take your product if it was free.

The Market For Your Product Or Service

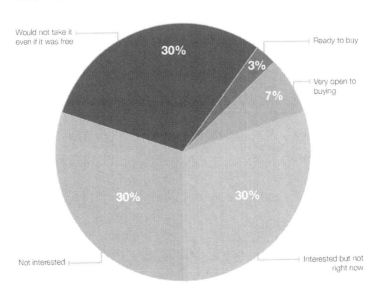

If you tried selling directly from your ad, you'd be targeting only the 3% who are ready to buy immediately and losing the other 97%.

By creating a lead generating ad, you increase your addressable market to 40%. You do this by capturing the 3% who are immediate buyers but also by capturing the 7% who are open to talking as well as the 30% who are interested but not right now.

By going from a 3% addressable market to 40%, you're increasing the effectiveness of your advertising by 1,233%.

This also has a secondary side effect with the people who are ready to buy immediately. They see you're not desperate to sell or discount your product or service. They see that you are interested in building a relationship first rather than just going for the jugular to make a sale. This kind of marketing is similar to sowing seeds on a farm. It is an investment in your future because as your database of interested prospects grows, so will your business and your results.

When you educate and teach you are seen as an expert and an authority. You're no longer questioned, instead you are obeyed and seen to have a personal, genuine, helpful interest in other people.

A sample campaign might have an offer of a free report or video series promising to educate your clients about the things they need to be aware of, how to avoid being ripped off and what they should look for. Once your prospect receives the value-packed information, you've delivered on all the promises made in your advertisement.

This skyrockets your trustworthiness, positions you as the expert and sets you apart from your competition. You haven't put sales pressure into your ad just to make a quick sale. Instead you're just starting with the process of getting them to raise their hand. You're asking them to contact you just so they identify themselves to you.

Managing Your Goldmine

As a kid I used to watch the futuristic cartoon *The Jetsons*. I was sure by the time I grew up we'd all be riding around in flying cars. Well according to my wife I have yet to grow up but nevertheless many years later my primary form of transport remains terrestrial.

Sure modern cars have some nice bells and whistles, but in their basic form and function cars haven't really changed in over one hundred years. So that begs the question, why aren't we all zipping around in personal flying machines?

Personal flight technology has been around for some time and the cost of it is surprisingly low. In mass production it would certainly come pretty close to what cars cost. So what's the problem? The short answer is there's simply no infrastructure to support personal flight. The vast majority of our infrastructure is built around cars. Modern houses, buildings and cities are all built to accommodate cars.

Why do some businesses get a constant flow of leads and prospects while others struggle to get any? The answer is the same as the answer to our personal flight dilemma—infrastructure.

Some businesses have built a marketing infrastructure which constantly brings in new leads, follows them up, nurtures and converts them into raving fan customers. Other businesses, in fact I would say most businesses, do what I call "random acts of marketing." They throw up an ad here, an ad there, perhaps a website or a brochure. They're not building infrastructure—a system whereby a cold lead enters one end and a raving fan customer comes out of the other.

These sporadic, one shot, random acts of marketing usually end up costing more than they bring in, which is demoralizing and sometimes leads business owners to say ridiculous things like "marketing doesn't work in my industry."

To build a **system**, we need to think it through from start to end. We need to understand how it works and what resources we'll need to run it.

At the absolute center of your marketing infrastructure is your database of customers and prospects, but to manage your database effectively you really need a CRM system. The CRM system is your marketing nerve center. It's where you manage your goldmine.

You want all your leads, all your customer interactions to end up in your CRM. This is where things get exciting.

Chapter 4 Action Item:
What Is Your Lead Capture System?
Fill in square #4 of your 1-Page Marketing Plan

Chapter 5

Nurturing Leads

Chapter 5 Summary

Nurturing leads is the process of taking people from being vaguely interested in what you have to offer to desiring it and wanting to do business with you. The lead nurturing process ensures that leads are interested, motivated, qualified and predisposed to buying from you before you ever try to sell to them.

Highlights covered in this chapter include:

- The secret behind the *Guinness World Records'* "world's greatest salesman."
- Why the money is in the follow-up and how to leverage this.
- How to annihilate your competitors and put yourself in a class of your own.
- A simple strategy for quickly moving prospects further into the buying cycle.
- Why a "marketing infrastructure" is critical to your business success and how to create one.
- The three major types of people you need in your team to make your business work.
- How to leverage international talent to ensure your business success.

The Secret Behind World's Greatest Salesman

Joe Girard is listed in the *Guinness World Records* as "the world's greatest salesman." He's sold more retail big ticket items, one at a time, than any other salesperson in recorded history. Was he selling some amazing new technology that everyone had to have? No. Was he selling to the mega rich? Wrong again. He sold ordinary cars to ordinary people. Between 1963 and 1978, he sold over 13,000 cars at a Chevrolet dealership. His stats are amazing:

- In total, he sold 13,001 cars. That's an average of six cars per day.
- On his best day, he sold 18 vehicles.
- On his best month, he sold 174.
- In his best year, he sold 1,425.
- Joe Girard sold more cars by himself than 95 percent of all the **dealerships** in North America.
- To make his feat even more incredible, he sold them at retail— one vehicle at a time. No bulk fleet deals.

So what was the secret to Joe's success? He lists several including working hard and being likeable. Without discounting these factors, I'm sure there were thousands of salesmen at that time who had those admirable qualities but they didn't sell a fraction of the volume that Joe did. One of the stand out things that Joe did was to constantly keep in touch with his customers. He sent a personalized greeting card **every month** to his entire list of customers. In January, it would be a Happy New Year card and inside it would say, "I like you." He would then sign his name and stamp it with the details of the dealership where he worked. In February, his list might get a Valentine's Day card. Again inside the message was the same, "I like you."

He would vary the size and color of the envelope and each was hand-addressed and stamped. This was critical to getting past the postal mail equivalent of spam filters, where people stand over the trash can and discard all the items that look like ads, scams, credit card offers and other types of junk mail. He wanted his customers to open his envelope, see his name and the positive message inside and feel good. He did this month after month, year after year in the knowledge that they would eventually need a new car. And when they did who do you think would have been top of mind? By the end of his career, he was sending out 13,000 cards per month and needed to hire an assistant to help him.

By the time he was a decade into his career, almost two-thirds of his sales were to repeat customers. It got to the point where customers had to set appointments in advance to come in and buy from him. Contrast that with other car salespeople who just stood around waiting and hoping for walk-in traffic.

Marketing Like A Farmer

What would you guess the average number of times a salesperson follows up a lead? If you guessed once or twice you'd be about right.

50% of salespeople give up after one contact, 65% give up after two and 79.8% give up after three shots[6]. Imagine that a farmer planted seeds and then refused to water them more than once or twice. Would he have a successful harvest? Hardly.

When it comes to marketing, **the money is in the follow-up**. Based on this we build the irresistible lead nurturing model.

---

[6] These statistics are widely quoted in sales and marketing circles. I attempted to track down the original source of these figures but after a few hours of research the best I could do was find was that they were "based on the findings of major national research firms." As with most statistics you should take them with a grain of salt. However, regardless of source or how these specific numbers were derived, in my experience they are about right. The point being that very few salespeople bother to follow up more than a few times.

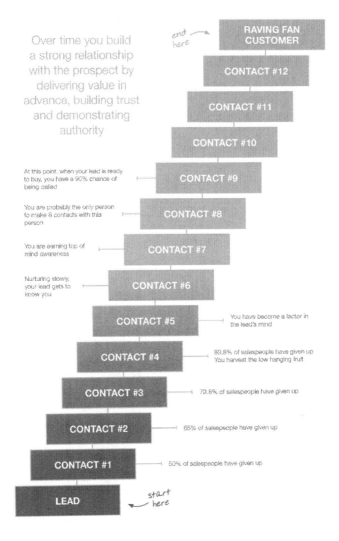

Over time you build a strong relationship with the prospect by delivering value in advance, building trust and demonstrating authority

end here

RAVING FAN CUSTOMER

CONTACT #12

CONTACT #11

CONTACT #10

At this point, when your lead is ready to buy, you have a 90% chance of being called

CONTACT #9

You are probably the only person to make 8 contacts with this person

CONTACT #8

You are earning top of mind awareness

CONTACT #7

Nurturing slowly, your lead gets to know you

CONTACT #6

CONTACT #5

You have become a factor in the lead's mind

CONTACT #4

89.8% of salespeople have given up
You harvest the low hanging fruit

CONTACT #3

79.5% of salespeople have given up

CONTACT #2

65% of salespeople have given up

CONTACT #1

50% of salespeople have given up

LEAD

start here

Immediately after you've captured a lead, they should go into your system where repeated contacts are made over time. These are not contacts where you obnoxiously try to pester them into buying. You build a relationship, giving them value in advance of them buying anything from you and in the process building trust and demonstrating authority in your field of expertise.

Accept the fact most people will not be ready to buy right away. Put them in a database—and by database this could be email or physical direct mail (preferably both). Mail them something regularly to stay in touch, positioning yourself as an expert in your industry or field (more on that in the next chapter).

Like a farmer you prepare your prospects to become ready for harvesting. Just as Joe Girard did, over time you too can build a huge pipeline of potential customers who'll have you at top of mind when **they're** ready to buy. Even more exciting is that they'll already be predisposed to doing business with you because of the value you've created in advance. You won't need to convince or put on a hard sell, the sale just becomes the next logical step.

This growing list of prospects and the relationship you have with them will become the most valuable asset in your business. It's the golden goose. Now when the prospect is finally ready to buy, you're a welcome invited guest rather than a pest. The most important thing you can take away from this message is to become a marketing farmer. It's a simple three step process:

1. Advertise with the intention of finding people who are interested in what you do. Do this by offering a free report, video, CD, etc. Any kind of relevant, free information that presents a solution to a problem they have will work. This positions you as an expert and as an educator rather than a salesperson. Which would **you** prefer to buy from?
2. Add them to your database.
3. Continually nurture them and provide them with value. For example, a newsletter on your industry or information on how to get the most from whatever it is you do or offer. Important point—do not make this a constant sales pitch. That will become old very quickly. Be sure to offer them valuable information with an occasional pitch or special offer. Most important of all, be sure to keep in contact regularly, otherwise the prospect will forget you and your relationship will then be relegated to that of a cold prospect and pest salesperson.

If you become a "marketing farmer," you'll have a rich and continual harvest as your database grows in number and quality.

Building Your Marketing Infrastructure

In the previous chapter we introduced the concept of advertising with the intention of capturing leads. Capturing leads is one thing but what you do with these leads is what really separates the boys from the men, so to speak. Have you ever had the experiencing of inquiring about a product or service and never receiving any follow-up? Or perhaps you received a quote and got one lazy follow-up call and nothing further? This is a sign of a broken marketing infrastructure.

The sad thing is that a lot, even most, of the follow-up grunt work can be automated using a CRM system. Most good CRM systems can be set up to automatically fire off an email or SMS to a client or alert a salesperson to call and follow up. The automation can be triggered based on some action taken by the prospect, by tracking inquiries and purchases or based on preset timers. Automation systems allow you to robotically sort, sift and screen prospects and customers so that you can leverage your time more effectively.

Now that you have a database of high probability prospects, **your job is to market to them until they buy or die**. It may seem like I'm advocating being obnoxious and pestering people to buy until they cave in. Nothing could be further from the truth.

Traditional selling training often focuses on pressure tactics like "always be closing" and other silly little close techniques which are based on pressure. It makes the seller a pest who the prospect wants to avoid.

Instead of being a pest, I advocate becoming a welcome guest. Send your high probability prospects a continuous stream of value until **they're** ready to buy. This could be in the form of tutorials, articles, case studies or even something as simple as a monthly newsletter that's related to their area of interest. This builds trust, goodwill and positions you as an expert and educator rather than just a sales person going for the jugular.

Various technology tools make it easy to automate this continuous follow-up mechanism, making this a cost effective and scalable way of building up a huge pipeline of interested and motivated prospects.

Some of these prospects will convert into customers immediately, while others will do so weeks, months or even years later. The point is that by the time they're ready to buy, you've already built a solid relationship with them based on value and trust. This makes you the logical choice when it comes time for them to make a buying decision.

This is one of the most ethical and painless ways of selling, because it's based completely on trust and an exchange of value. While your competitors are blindly shooting arrows every which way in the hope of hitting one of the 3% of immediate buyers, with this technique you're focusing all of your firepower on a clear and visible target.

Your marketing infrastructure will be made up of "assets." Here are a few of the assets I've successfully deployed in marketing infrastructures that I've built or helped manage:

- Lead capture websites
- Free recorded message info lines
- Newsletters
- Blogs
- Free reports
- Direct mail sequences
- Email sequences
- Social media
- Online videos and DVDs
- Podcasts and Audio CDs
- Print ads
- Hand written notes
- Email auto-responders
- SMS auto-responders
- Shock and awe packages (discussed in the next section)

These are all part of my marketing infrastructure. I continue to build bigger and more sophisticated assets but these are some of which make up my core. Each one of these has a place and purpose. All the ads that I run are designed to plug cold leads into this system and convert them to raving fan customers.

Of course it does take time and money to build such a marketing infrastructure, but just like building physical infrastructure like roads or a railway network—the bulk of the time and cost goes into the initial build. After that it's just maintenance.

And here's the exciting thing—thanks to advances in technology, much of my marketing system is automated, which gives me enormous leverage. When I find a combination that works, I can redeploy it over and over and reliably get the same results.

As I continue to build out my marketing infrastructure, my results continue to improve. What about you? Are you building your marketing infrastructure? Are you constantly building on and improving your marketing systems?

Doing so is what will put you far ahead of your competitors who'll be just fluffing about with their random acts of marketing.

Lumpy Mail And The Shock And Awe Package

In Chapter 3 we discussed the power of postal mail as a media channel. "Lumpy mail" is a way of taking this powerful media channel and putting it on steroids. Think about your postal mail sorting habits. You have a pile of envelopes then you notice one of the envelopes has something in it that makes it lumpy. There's a 3D physical object in it, perhaps a book, DVD or a trinket of some sort. Which of your envelopes is going to get opened first and get the most attention? If you're like most people it will be the lumpy one.

Lumpy mail is an attention getter and allows you to get very creative with your direct mail campaigns. In the direct mail industry, trinkets purposely inserted for attracting attention are called "grabbers." Grabbers often set the theme of your sales letter. For example you might insert a small plastic trash can into the envelope with the theme of the sales letter being, "Stop Wasting Money." Or perhaps you insert a magnet with the theme being, "Attract More Clients." It sounds corny and it probably is, but it gets attention, entertains and more importantly if done right, it gets great results.

Books, CDs and DVDs are other excellent items you can insert in envelopes to make them lumpy. Other than just attracting attention once off when being opened, these items generally don't get thrown away. Your customers and prospects will likely keep what you sent them indefinitely and it will be a constant reminder of you.

Taking lumpy mail to the next level is the "shock and awe package.[7]" The shock and awe package is perhaps one of the most powerful direct response marketing follow-up tools in existence. When done right it can skyrocket conversions and position you far above your competitors. In fact, it's so powerful it essentially annihilates your competitors and puts you in a class of your own. The awesome thing about them is that even when your competitors find out what you're doing, they usually won't dare copy you. Practically no one does this.

In the previous chapter we discussed the importance of capturing the details of prospects who have indicated interest. The purpose of this of course is to keep in touch with them and nurture them to the point where they're ready to become a customer.

Now think back to the last time you enquired about a product or service. Perhaps you phoned in, emailed or submitted your inquiry through a web page. You did the typical prospect dance of "send me more information." What did you get back in response to this request? Likely the organization you were inquiring with did one of the following things:

- Sent you a link to a web page
- Sent you an email (perhaps accompanied by some attachments)
- Spoke with you over the phone and answered your questions

It may have been all or some of the above. See what's happening? They're responding to your inquiry in the cheapest and most efficient manner. There's nothing wrong with cheap and efficient but no one is going to be entertained, delighted or inspired by it. No one's going to stop and say, "Wow they sent me a PDF file with all the specifications, how awesome!"

With your first few interactions with prospects you have the opportunity to make one of the following three impressions:

---

[7] The name and concept is generally credited as being the invention of direct marketing legend Dan Kennedy

1. same same
2. crappy
3. mind-blowingly amazing

Most business owners choose option 1, a surprisingly large number choose option 2 and almost no one chooses option 3. Your job is to devise a way to be option 3. Fortunately you don't need to reinvent the wheel. A "shock and awe package" is one of the best ways to do this.

A shock and awe package is essentially a physical box that you mail or deliver to prospects full of unique benefit-laden assets related to your business and industry. Here are some of the things you can and should include in a shock and awe package:

- Books—people are conditioned to almost never throw books out. Big bonus points if it's a book you wrote. Books are an amazing positioning tool and catapult you from salesperson to educator and expert authority instantly. I'm doing this right now with this book! :-)
- DVDs or CDs introducing yourself and the specific problems your product, service or business solves for your prospect.
- Testimonials from past clients in video, audio or written form.
- Clippings from media mentions or features about you, your product or industry
- Brochures, sales letters or other marketing material
- Independent reports or whitepapers proving your point or demonstrating the value of your type of product or service.
- A sample of your products or services. Coupons or gift cards with a face value on them can be powerful as it feels like "wasting money" to just throw these out. They also motivate the prospect to try you out.
- Unusual trinkets and gifts that entertain, inform and wow. I've heard of everything from personalized coffee mugs to iPads being included.
- Handwritten notes thanking them for inquiring or recapping a conversation you've had with them over the phone.

Whaaaat?, I hear you say. Snail mail in this instant access, on-demand, "information age?" The answer is YES! Trust me, no one loves technology more than I do. I'm a sucker for the latest iAnything and I'm constantly glued to one of many screens. However, like most people I love receiving packages—even more so when they're unexpected.

While people's snail mail used to be much more voluminous, it's now easier than ever to get cut through with physical mail and especially packages. If something in a FedEx box lands on your desk how long is it before you rip it open? If you're like most people, I suspect it's not very long.

I'm certainly not saying you shouldn't send immediate responses to information inquiries using the phone, email or web but understand that the first few interactions with a prospect are sacred and should be carefully orchestrated. Nothing should be left to chance. A shock and awe pack is an amazing tool for delivering that "wow" emotion in your prospect.

A shock and awe pack should do three things:

- Give your prospect amazing, unexpected value
- Position you as an expert and trusted authority in your field
- Move your prospect further down the buying cycle than they would otherwise have been

How much more powerful is this than the standard "Sure, I'll shoot an email with more information."

A common objection to shock and awe packages is that they're too expensive. In the previous chapter we discussed that, all other things being equal, the more money you can spend marketing to high probability prospects, the better your chances are of converting them to a customer. That's what the shock and awe pack is all about. If you can outspend your competitor wooing and wowing prospects, you'll run rings around them. Of course **you must know your numbers**, particularly numbers like customer lifetime value otherwise you will go negative. **You can't substitute good marketing for bad maths**.

The numbers obviously have to make sense. Unless you're in an extremely low margin, purely transactional business (something I really don't recommend you be in) then the numbers should work and sending the shock and awe pack should be very economical.

Don't make the mistake of being cheap and efficient when it comes to wooing prospects. Shock and awe packages are a huge competitive advantage. Most competitors won't understand them and even those who do, usually won't have the courage to use them because, if they're like most businesses, they won't know their numbers. They will likely perceive them as being too expensive—after all there are cheaper and more efficient ways to acquire customers. Let your competitors do cheap and efficient marketing while yours entertains, delights, inspires and wows. It will put you worlds apart.

Become A Prolific Marketer

One of the commonalities amongst high growth businesses is that they focus heavily on marketing and make a lot of offers. Some of these offers end up being misses and some end up being hits. The exciting part is that you don't need many hits to offset your misses, especially if you place "small bets" by first testing with a small segment of your list.

By making many offers, you start to get a very good sense of what works and what doesn't. When you become a prolific marketer it's much easier to spot trends and scientifically measure response by split testing.

Another important attribute of high growth businesses is that they're not timid with their offers. They take risks, use compelling copy and make outrageous guarantees.

Could it really be that simple? Making more compelling and more frequent offers? The short answer is yes. The fundamentals never change. Sure there are now more media channels through which to make offers, new marketing technology to help you track return on investment and split test, but the fundamentals never change.

More compelling and more frequent offers = rapid business growth.

Being more prolific with your marketing will create a buzz in your business. Your clients and prospects will start to notice you more and you'll start to cut through the clutter and fill up your sales pipeline.

Any change that becomes part of your routine, whether positive or negative, will have a profound impact over time. If you make the crafting and sending offers to your list of clients and prospects part of your regular routine, within a short time you'll have a dramatically different business.

Making regular offers will make you a better marketer. Getting good at the science of marketing is the key to rapid business growth. And when you get better, everything will get better for you.

Make It Up, Make It Real and Make It Recur

In school, you were taught to be independent. You had to pass math, science and English to get to the next level. Imagine you pooled your talents with a couple of friends. One friend who was good at math did all the math tests. Another friend who was good at science did all the science tests. Finally, you did all the English tests, because that's what you were good at. In school, that type of collaborative work structure would have been called cheating and all three of you might have been disciplined or even expelled. Yet in business, pooling different talents in pursuit of a single goal is exactly the type of structure that results in successful outcomes. Business is a team sport. One where you're never going to win on your own.

It takes different "types" to make a business work. Here are the three major types that it takes:

- **The Entrepreneur** - This is the ideas person or visionary. They see a problem or gap in the market and are willing to take risks so they can solve that problem for a profit. **They make it up**. E.g. Seeing a gap in the market for a particular product and hiring all the right people needed to get it up and running.
- **The Specialist** - This is an implementer of your vision. They could be an engineer, a venture capitalist, a graphic designer. They take your vision, or part of it, and help make it reality. **They make it real**. e.g. Building the factory to produce the product, getting the tooling right, creating the product packaging.

- **The Manager** - They come in every day and make sure things get done, work gets delivered and the vision is on track. **They make it recur**. Running the factory, making sure shipments get out on time, making sure quality is right.

It takes all three types for business success yet it's extremely rare for a single person to be good at all three. Many small business owners are either the Entrepreneur or the Specialist or both but rarely the Manager.

Even if you're currently the sole operator of your business, you need to find a way to have all three bases covered. You can do this by outsourcing or hiring. Small business owners often try to take on too much and things inevitably slip through the gaps. Lack of a Manager role is often why a marketing infrastructure never gets up and running properly. It's why monthly newsletters don't go out or why shock and awe packs never get sent. The business owner might agree these are great lead nurturing ideas (and they are) but they're busy being the Entrepreneur or Specialist and in the absence of a Manager taking care of the marketing infrastructure, they don't get done.

So what's the point of having sophisticated marketing tools and assets like a shock and awe pack if they don't consistently get deployed?

You've probably already got all three roles handled in many other parts of your business. For example when you were starting out, you had the idea and vision for what you were going to build—you made it up. You then might have hired a lawyer to set up the business's legal structure—your lawyer made it real. Then every year you might get your accountant to take care of your tax returns and compliance—your accountant makes it recur.

It's critical you do the same for your marketing infrastructure. Get systems into place (we talk more about systems in Chapter 7). Come up with the marketing ideas or better still, shamelessly steal the ones in this book, hire graphic designers, web developers and copywriters to make it real, then get admin help or use fulfillment services to make it recur. As discussed earlier, much of this can be automated and what can't be automated should be delegated. It's just too important to neglect. Lack of a functional, running, marketing infrastructure will harm or possibly kill your business.

The reason you likely don't neglect your annual tax obligations is because it's enforced upon you by the government. They have a calendar which dictates when tax returns needs to be filed and when various taxes need to be paid.

You can replicate a similar forcing mechanism with a "marketing calendar." A marketing calendar sets out what marketing activities have to happen on a daily, weekly, monthly, quarterly and annual basis and you put those into your schedule like you would any other important business events.

For example, you might decide the following marketing calendar is right for your business:

- **Daily:** Check social media for mentions and respond appropriately.
- **Weekly:** Write a blog post and send the link in an email blast to email list subscribers.
- **Monthly:** Mail customers and prospects a printed newsletter or postcard.
- **Quarterly:** Send past customers who haven't purchased recently a reactivation letter.
- **Annually:** Send all customers a gift basket thanking them for their business.

After you've locked in **what** needs to be done and **when**, the only other question you need to answer is **who** will be responsible for delivering on each of these scheduled marketing activities. Again if you're a small or sole operator don't try and do it all yourself. Where possible make these repetitive operational activities someone else's responsibility.

In addition to regular, scheduled marketing activities, you need to consider event triggered marketing activities. For example, consider these event triggers and their corresponding actions:

- **You meet a potential prospect at a business event:** Transcribe their details from their business card into your CRM system and put them on your monthly newsletter/postcard list.
- **You get an inbound sales inquiry:** Send them a handwritten note and your shock and awe package.

- **You get a new email list subscriber from your blog:** Add them to your CRM system which automatically emails them an educational five-part video series over the next thirty days.
- **Received a customer complaint:** After the issue is resolved send them a handwritten apology note and a $100 discount coupon on their next purchase.

Again as far as possible make these event triggered activities someone else's responsibility. This will free you up to do higher level marketing tasks like designing and testing new marketing campaigns or improving the value of your offering. There are few business activities that pay as highly as working **on** your marketing.

Even if your business is currently small, hire admin help in the form of a manager type who will "run the factory" for you and make sure your scheduled and event triggered marketing activities recur.

As entrepreneurs we have a "can do" mindset. This often means when something needs to be done, we are tempted to just roll up our sleeves and just do it. However, spending a lot of time doing things that aren't your area of expertise or aren't a good use of your time can quickly become a very expensive exercise. Remember money is a renewable resource—you can always get more money but you can never get more time.

Another common concern with outsourcing or delegating tasks is quality. Will they get done as well as if you were doing them yourself? The answer is probably not, but a rule of thumb I like to use is **if someone else can do it 80% as good as you can, then you should delegate it**.

Letting go can be difficult, especially if you're a control freak and perfectionist like most entrepreneurial types are. But it's necessary if you're going to get scalability and leverage in your business. Otherwise you end up effectively paying yourself minimum wage for routine tasks while sacrificing high value tasks such as building your marketing infrastructure, which can take your business to a whole new level.

Some timeless wisdom from Jim Rohn:

Learn how to separate the majors and the minors. A lot of people don't do well simply because they major in minor things.

Don't mistake movement for achievement. It's easy to get faked out by being busy. The question is: Busy doing what?

Days are expensive. When you spend a day you have one less day to spend. So make sure you spend each one wisely.

We can no more afford to spend major time on minor things than we can to spend minor time on major things.

Time is more valuable than money. You can get more money, but you cannot get more time.

Time is the best-kept secret of the rich.

Finally the most common complaint is that it's too expensive to hire or outsource help. This may have been true a few years ago but not any more thanks to the wonder of geoarbitrage. There is an enormous pool of talent in Southeast Asia, India and Eastern Europe that will work for you at a fraction of the price of local employees and contractors.

There's a good reason large companies move a lot of their routine operations to these locations. They are full of workers who are talented, eager, well-educated and speak English fluently.

You can assign tasks and have them magically happen while you sleep. Importantly, it's not just about cost but also about scalability. Locally you would need to comply with all sorts of red tape when hiring and firing employees or even contractors. However, thanks to massive online job boards like Upwork, Freelancer and 99Designs you can hire an army of personal assistants, graphic designers, web developers and almost any other skill you can imagine. All of these can be hired on demand to work on a project basis or as part of your team on an ongoing basis

The production of this book is a perfect example of this. It was written by me in Australia, edited by a copy editor based in the United States who works for an Armenian company. The cover design was done by a graphic designer in India and my researcher was based in the Philippines. The Internet has broken down geographical barriers and enabled anyone to have a global workforce. Never before has so much talent been so readily available and been so cost effective.

Of course from time to time the tired old argument about patriotism and creating local jobs comes up, but how many local jobs are you going to create if you fail to implement critical marketing strategies and go out of business? Globalization of labor and talent is a reality and has been for some time. Previously the domain of only large multinational companies, it's now in easy reach of small to medium businesses and entrepreneurs like you and I. This is a real game changer. As entrepreneurs, our job is to embrace change and find ways to leverage and profit from it, rather than fight it.

As you become more successful you'll help create local jobs as a byproduct of your success. When you upgrade your house, give generously to a good cause or buy a new car, you'll be creating local jobs and benefiting your local community, most of which wouldn't have been possible if your business had failed.

<u>Chapter 5 Action Item:</u>
What Is Your Lead Nurturing System?
Fill in square #5 of your 1-Page Marketing Plan

Chapter 6

Sales Conversion

Chapter 6 Summary

Sales conversion is all about creating enough trust and demonstrating enough value to motivate interested leads to become paying customers. Positioning yourself correctly will make the sales conversion process easy and natural for both you and your customer.

Highlights covered in this chapter include:

- Why positioning is the critical factor when it comes to charging high prices for your products and services.
- How to position yourself as a welcome guest rather than a pest when selling.
- Why the odds are stacked against you if you're a small to medium business and what to do to level the playing field.
- How to massively reduce the perceived risk that customers see when it comes to buying from you.
- How to instantly generate trust and credibility when selling.
- How to correctly price your products and services.
- How to remove the roadblocks that are preventing people from buying.

Every Dog Bites

You've likely heard the corny old joke, which appears in the classic movie, *The Pink Panther Strikes Again*. There Peter Sellers who plays the hapless Inspector Clouseau sees a cute dog and in his ridiculous French accent asks the man standing near it, "Does your dog bite?" The man shakes his head and replies, "No." Clouseau then reaches out to pat the dog whereupon the dog lashes out and bites his hand. He then turns back to the man and indignantly asks, "I thought you said your dog didn't bite?" The man casually replies, "That is not my dog."

The people you're selling to have been bitten too many times and now think all dogs bite. The fact is unless you're the well-known incumbent in your industry, you're not even starting the selling process in neutral territory but rather you're starting behind in negative territory. Even though you're an ethical operator, your prospects are cynical and don't trust you. Unfortunately it's a case of guilty until proven innocent and you have to work your way from negative to positive territory and win their trust before a sale can be made.

With trust being **the** major barrier to a sale you've got to have some solid strategies for sales conversion. While a comprehensive program of sales training[8] is out of the scope of this book, in this chapter we're going to look at a few strategies and tactics that will make the sales conversion process much easier. Specifically we're going to discuss the central role played by positioning and how to make proper positioning a part of your trust-based sales conversion process.

In the previous two chapters we covered how to capture and nurture high probability leads in order to build trust, value and authority. All this was done with the purpose of making the sales conversion process natural and easy. By the time you get them to the point of sales conversion, they should already be pre-framed, pre-motivated and pre-interested and essentially **asking** to buy from you. If you have to convince them or put on the hard sell then you likely need to improve your lead nurturing process.

---

[8] For a comprehensive study of modern selling strategies I highly recommend *SPIN Selling* by Neil Rackham

Most sales people position themselves either as desperate beggars or as obnoxious, pushy sales people using silly outdated "closing" techniques like ABC (always be closing), the trial close or the assumptive close. These techniques have become a joke in selling and unless you're selling low-value products like vacuum cleaners door-to-door, they'll create more distrust with your prospect rather than help you.

Another equally bad approach taken in many new businesses is expecting sales to happen by the mere fact that they exist. Some open a physical store, others start a website and expect sales to just start rolling in. Their marketing strategy is hope. And sure they may make a small number of sales just by virtue of being there when a random prospect wanders by. But that is a guaranteed path to frustration. Many such businesses make just enough in sales to torture themselves to death. They then conclude the market or their industry is too competitive.

Truth be told, I don't know of any market or industry that is not competitive. But one thing I know for certain is that in any market or industry you look at, no matter how competitive, there'll be someone doing really well and there'll be someone struggling.

So if we were honest with ourselves, we couldn't really put it down to a problem with the market or industry. So what's the problem? The problem is likely that they're positioning themselves as a commodity, a "me too" type of business.

When you position yourself in this way you're only marketing weapons are to shout as loudly as possible (which is very expensive) or to discount your prices as far as possible (which is dangerous). Unless you are a Costco, Walmart or other such behemoth, you really don't want price to be your key differentiator, as that's a battle you won't win.

At this stage many of these businesses realize their folly and start making dubious and unquantifiable claims like being "the best," "the highest quality," etc.

There's No Money In Your Product Or Service

Whether you're selling freshly baked bread, accounting services or IT support, the way you market yourself will have a dramatic impact on the clients you attract and the amount that you can charge for your services. A commonly held belief is that "it's all about the product" so if you have a better product or service people will automatically be more likely to buy from you and pay you more for it.

While this is true to some extent, the law of diminishing returns comes into play when your product or service reaches a "good enough" level. After all, how much better can your IT support or accounting services or bread be than that of your competition? Once you've reached a level of competence, **the real profit comes from the way you market yourself**.

How much does a world class violinist make? Well that depends on how he markets himself. Have you ever heard of Joshua Bell? He's one of the finest classical musicians in the world. He plays to packed audiences all around the world, making upwards of $1,000 per minute. The violin that he plays is a Stradivarius violin built in 1713, currently valued at $3.5 million. This particular Stradivarius violin, being close to 300 years old, is renowned to be the most beautiful sounding violin ever crafted.

So, here we have the finest violinist in the world playing the most beautiful violin ever. It's safe to say that Bell, as a musician, is the best at what he does. At the height of his career he was approached by the *Washington Post* to participate in a social experiment. They wanted him to play at a local subway for an hour, during which thousands of people would walk by and hear him playing. So on the morning of January 12, 2007, Bell played through a set list of classical masterpieces with his violin case open. Can you a guess how much the finest violinist in the world, playing a beautiful $3.5 million violin made in hour? A grand total of $32.

To see the video of the Joshua Bell social experiment visit 1pmp.com

---

The finest violinist, playing the most beautiful instrument made a meager $32 from his "customers." The same violinist played in a Boston concert hall a few nights earlier. It was a performance where audience members paid $100 or more per ticket. During that event, he earned over $60,000 per hour.

The same talented musician, playing the same music on the same violin, yet in one instance he earns $32 an hour and in another, he earns $60,000 per hour. What made the dramatic difference? In a word—positioning.

If you're a professional musician and you position yourself as a subway busker, your "customers" will treat you as such and pay you accordingly. Conversely if you position yourself as a professional concert performer you attract a totally different customer and once again get paid accordingly. In other words, people will generally take you at your own appraisal—unless proven otherwise.

Of course you can't cheat by positioning yourself as a professional musician and then show up and be unable to perform at a high level. The same is true regardless what business you're in. If you've got a quality product or service, what's stopping you from positioning it at a much higher level—offering it a premium price and attracting a much higher quality of customer?

Resolve to stop positioning yourself as a commodity and competing solely on price. The result to your bottom line will be phenomenal.

Transitioning From Pest To Welcome Guest

How do you feel about a dear friend who shows up at your front door? Contrast this with how you feel about a stranger selling door-to-door who interrupts your dinner or family time. What's the difference? The former is a welcome guest, someone you have a relationship and connection with. The latter is a pest. You don't know who he is, where he's from and most likely you don't even want or need what he's selling.

The welcome guest brings value to your life, whereas the pest is just there to interrupt you and to take. Wouldn't it be great if you could approach a prospect and be treated by them as a welcome guest rather than a pest? Selling suddenly becomes much easier and more pleasant when you are welcomed with open arms and when the prospect is deeply interested in what you have to offer. This is the transformation I'd like you to make in your business and in your marketing. Transition from being a pest to a welcome guest.

Most businesses try to sell without first creating trust. They either cold call or advertise using outdated methods that no longer work.

The problem with this is you're asking your customer to make a decision when they have no idea about who you are or what you're about. They don't know you, don't like you and don't trust you yet.

It's like proposing marriage on a first date—sure it may work once in a blue moon but do you really want to stake your whole business on a strategy like that? And so you end up with a poor closing ratio of say 1 in 10 or 1 in 20 and you waste a significant amount of time, energy and money dealing with unqualified prospects. What's more, you waste a lot of money on poor advertising.

You have a generic ad and you get people calling up and you say to them, "Sure I can come out and see you" or "Sure I can help you." The problem with this is they barely know you and are probably just price shopping, so your conversion is probably going to be at a far lower level than it could be.

At this stage many business owners get hooked on the "hopeium" drug. Hopeium is a "drug" that travels through your body and mind when you "think" you have an interested prospect who is sending you positive signals but has no intention of buying from you. The drug is usually activated when your prospect tells you "Tell me more about your product…" "Send me a quote…" or "Send me more information……" You know what I mean right? Someone calls your office and shows interest in what you have to offer and then instantaneously you feel the "rush" of excitement that this is going to be your next sale.

Then a few days or a few weeks later after continually chasing them, you get hit with the "silent treatment." You've had some good conversations and they've expressed interest in what you have to offer then all of a sudden everything stops and goes cold. You try calling them back once or twice. You even send a follow-up email, but nothing. They just disappear. You figure you've somehow lost the sale, and you don't know what you did wrong, or what was wrong with your product. It makes selling feel like such a painful and arduous process.

Hopeium is dangerous because it's not based on the truth of what your prospect is really thinking. The faster you "detox" from hopeium, the sooner you'll stop wasting your selling time chasing prospects who aren't a true fit for your solution.

Over the years, clients have become more and more skeptical. They've been burnt too many times and they simply don't believe you. So the problem is you're not even starting at zero, you're starting in negative territory. And the old school "close, close, close... sell, sell, sell" approach doesn't work the way it used to. Potential clients get their back up and end up doing nothing because they don't trust you.

Instead you need to move towards the model of... educate, educate, educate. With education, you build trust. With education, you position yourself as an expert. With education you build relationships. With education you make the selling process easier for both buyer and seller.

As discussed in the previous chapter, instead of trying to sell to them straight off the bat, the first thing you do is offer your readers something of value that educates them about a problem they have. A free report, free CD, free DVD, online webinar, etc., are all great educational tools you can use.

Delaying the sale accomplishes two things. First, it shows you're willing to give long before you take, which breaks down sales resistance. Second, it presents you as an educator and expert in your field. Think about it. Who would you prefer to buy from—a pushy salesperson salivating for their next commission or an expert educator who has your interests at heart and wants to help you solve your problem?

You must stop selling and start educating, consulting and advising prospects about the benefits your products and services deliver as opposed to each and every competitor in your category.

Best you read that again, it could be worth a fortune to you.

Let's face it, no one wants to be seen as a stereotypical salesperson who is a pushy and untrustworthy. However, if you think about yourself as a doctor who diagnoses and then prescribes solutions to people's problems, then I'm sure you'd be much more comfortable selling under those circumstances—as a trusted, educated, knowledgeable, qualified, confident, capable adviser.

And that is exactly who you need to be perceived as in the eyes and mind of your prospects—someone who **educates** them and solves their problems.

This would be a good time to share with you my definition of an entrepreneur, "Someone who solves people's problems at a profit."

Bottom line, don't let them think you are in sales for one second. The best way to do all this is consultative, advisory selling using a nurturing system (more on that shortly). You must see yourself as an agent of change, a creator of great value, benefit and advantage in the lives of your customers and prospects.

Become the expert in your category or industry. Quite honestly, everybody is generally trying to be an expert, it's just their marketing sucks. The coffee shop is trying to make the best coffee, it just sucks at marketing that fact.

Consultative, advisory selling is the most cost effective, the most enduring, the most impactful and the most powerful marketing strategy a business owner could ever devise.

The balance of power is now in the hands of those who would choose to consult, advise and educate prospects or clients about the benefit that your product brings to them. It's the only way to take the power back off the buyer in the chaotic collaborative world we live in today. So stop selling and start educating and advising. Your clients will appreciate you more and so will your bank manager.

Manufacturing Trust

Ask most people and they'll tell you they despise dealing with large, dumb companies. Poor service, indifferent staff and out-of-touch management are hallmarks of large companies. Yet for some reason we keep dealing with them despite knowing that there are probably much better options out there.

One of the biggest reasons behind this is a comfort, that while the experience may not be great, it likely won't be horrible. As the saying goes, "Better the devil you know than the devil you don't." Fly by night operators and snake oil salesmen have made many people distrust small businesses by default. People know that while a large company might not give the very best service, they are unlikely to be outright scammed by them.

If you run a small business that puts you at an immediate disadvantage. A customer doing in-depth due diligence on you may come to the conclusion that you are trustworthy and provide great service, but the vast majority of customers won't go to that effort. They will often take a cursory glance and judge you by your cover.

That's why it's increasingly important to present your business in a way that conveys trust and confidence. The strategic use of technology is one way that you can level the playing field. In times not so long ago, access to business technology tools was cost prohibitive for small businesses and hence was the domain of large companies. The Internet, software as a service (SaaS) and cloud computing have leveled the playing field.

A famous cartoon published in *The New Yorker* depicts a dog sitting at a computer and is captioned, "On the Internet, nobody knows you're a dog." This illustrates how technology can help make the little guy look like one of the big guys—leveling the playing field and helping fight the trust bias against small businesses.

The following are some inexpensive ways you can use technology to help you present your business in a larger and more professional manner. Other than the fact they will help you fight the small business trust bias, many of these tools will help you run and scale your business in a much more efficient manner.

Website: Your website is probably one of the first places prospects go to check you out. Beware of the following signals which scream to potential prospects that you are small or potentially untrustworthy:

- No phone number listed. Phone numbers should be prominently listed at the top of every page.
- A PO Box address or no address listed instead of a proper physical business address. Even if you work from home, you can use virtual office services to meet with customers and to display a business address on your website.
- Lack of privacy policy and/or terms of use. Templates for these are widely available.

- Poor or cheap-looking design. Don't skimp on design, even if you build the website yourself, attractive easy-to-use website templates are available at very minimal cost.

Email Address: It amazes me how many small, even medium-sized businesses advertise a Hotmail, Gmail or ISP-issued email address rather than using an email address with their own domain. Who looks more trustworthy johnny14@gmail.com or john.smith@company.com?

Phone Number: Your phone number can say a lot about you. Using a national toll free number or a toll free word or "vanity" number can give your business a national and accessible feel. It can also help people recall your phone number on fast-moving mediums such as radio or billboards where the prospect has only a split second to take note of your phone number.

CRM: As discussed in previous chapters this is your marketing nerve center. A customer relationship management (CRM) system will help you keep track of customer details and automate and manage follow-up. It's a much more efficient way of managing customer records than just a spreadsheet or some ad-hoc filing system.

Ticketing System: If dealing with customer support or inquiries, a ticketing system can help you and your customers keep track of requests. This can dramatically lower the burden on you and your staff to respond to status updates, phone calls and emails. It also gives the potential customer confidence that their request is trackable and hasn't gone into some black hole.

These are just a few of the tools that can help you fight the trust bias that disadvantages small businesses. Using these tools you can punch above your weight and present yourself as a professional organization, even if you're just starting out.

While these tools are not a replacement for having great products and great service, they can help you manage perception. Keep focused on your marketing and soon perception will become reality.

Outrageous Guarantees

The first time I saw tasting spoons at an ice creamery, I finally realized just how truly risk averse we all are. Here potential ice cream buyers hold up a queue of people behind them while they taste test several flavors with tiny plastic spoons. All this is to ensure that the flavor of ice cream they finally commit to buying doesn't disappoint.

Risk reversal in form of an outrageous guarantee means that if the product or service doesn't work out for the prospect, you're the one who'll have something to lose rather than them. This needs to be more powerful than something ordinary and lame like "money back guarantee" or "satisfaction guaranteed." By having something to lose if it doesn't work out, you have an easier path to the sale and you'll much more easily avoid alarm bells set off in your prospect's brain.

Here's a practical example. If I'm wanting to hire an IT company for my business what sort of things might I fear? Here are a few that immediately come to mind:

- Are they going to send some junior technician who'll fluff about for hours as he learns on the job while I get billed a premium hourly rate for the privilege?
- Are they going to be available when I urgently need support?
- Will the problems they fix continue to recur?
- Are they going to bamboozle me with geek speak when I request an explanation of work performed or needed?

A risk reversal guarantee for this type of business might look like: "We guarantee that our certified and experienced IT consultants will fix your IT problems so they don't recur. They'll also return your calls within fifteen minutes and will always speak to you in plain English. If we don't live up to any of these promises, we insist that you tell us and we'll credit back to your account double the billable amount of the consultation." Compare that to a weak and vague guarantee like, "satisfaction guaranteed."

To be truly effective when using this technique you must avoid the vague crap that everyone says, e.g. satisfaction guaranteed, service, quality, dependability. Your guarantee should be very specific and address the fear or uncertainty that the prospect has about the transaction.

For example, if you're in the pest control business your customers want to know that:

- The pests won't come back
- The technician won't leave their house dirty
- You won't poison their family or pets with chemicals

So your outrageous guarantee could be something like this:

"We guarantee to rid your home of ants forever, without the use of toxic chemicals, while leaving your home in the same clean and tidy condition we found it. If you aren't absolutely delighted with the service provided, we insist that you tell us and we'll refund double your money back."

Is this kind of guarantee risky? Only if you consistently do a crappy job. If you are committed to giving your customers excellent service and training your staff accordingly, then there is almost zero risk for you. More importantly there's also almost zero risk for your prospects, which makes closing sales much easier. Indeed the law may even require that you provide warranties as to the quality of your products and services and make things right if they fall short. So given this is likely already a legal requirement, why not up the ante and make it a feature you promote in your marketing?

Here's the other thing about guarantees. If you're an ethical operator, you are most likely already offering a guarantee but you just aren't using it to your advantage in your marketing. So why not make a point of talking about something that you're already doing. Most people are honest and won't abuse guarantees if they've received the service they were promised. Even after accounting for the few people who do abuse them, you'll be far ahead because a strong guarantee will attract more customers than a weak and vague one.

A smart entrepreneur will look at their business from the eyes of a fearful, skeptical prospect and reverse all the perceived risks so that the path to the sale is much smoother. This also results in customers who are much more sticky and who won't fall for your competitors who by comparison seem much more risky to deal with.

A strong, results-oriented guarantee will also drive you to deliver a great customer experience. This alone ensures that it's worthwhile to have a strong guarantee. Your customers have their own fears. When you can name the fears and guarantee against them in your marketing, you give yourself an overwhelming advantage over your competitors.

Pricing Strategy

Setting price on your products or services is one of the weightiest decisions you'll make in your business. It will touch every part of your business from the financials to how you are perceived in the market place. Yet often scant attention is paid to the psychology and marketing potential of price.

The price of your product is a critical positioning indicator. Do you think when they go to set price on a Rolls Royce or Ferrari, they just add up the bill of materials and then just add on an acceptable markup? Hardly. Price is central to the positioning of the product.

As discussed earlier in this chapter, if you position yourself as an educator and a trusted adviser price becomes much more flexible. I hope you're never in unfortunate position of needing heart surgery but if you are do you want the cheapest heart surgeon? I doubt it.

More often than not, business owners set prices based on what their competitors charge. A common application of this is setting price slightly lower than the market leader in their industry. Another common way that price is set is to just take cost price and then add what feels like an acceptable markup.

Both of these are acceptable starting points; however, if you aren't thinking about the marketing or the psychological implications of price then you are likely leaving huge sums of money on the table.

Number Of Options

Regardless of industry, most products or services offer multiple flavors or variants of the primary offering. Henry Ford famously offered his customers the Model T "In any color that he wants so long as it is black."

While it may seem backward by today's expectations of infinite choice and expressions of individuality through ever increasing personalization, the great industrialist does bring up an issue that is relevant to all entrepreneurs. How much choice should we offer?

Conventional wisdom would have you believe that the more choice you offer, the more sales you will make. However, this has been proven totally false time and time again.

There is a famous study by a professor of business at Columbia University that illustrates this point well. In a California gourmet market, Professor Iyengar and her research assistants set up a booth of samples of jam. Every few hours, they switched between a selection of twenty-four flavors of jam to only six flavors. On average, customers tasted two jam flavors, regardless of the size of the assortment.

Here's the interesting part. Sixty percent of customers were drawn to the large assortment, while only forty percent stopped by the small one. But thirty percent of the people who had sampled from the small assortment decided to buy, while only three percent of those confronted with the flavors purchased a jar.

The conclusion? Offering too much choice can actually **prevent** sales. The psychology behind this finding is that people get caught like a deer in the headlights. Fear of making a suboptimal choice prevents them from making any choice at all.

If you look at Apple and their wildly successful products, you'll see they are usually offered in only two or three variations each. This seems to be the happy medium between too few options and the brain overload that is caused by too many options.

Along these lines, a pricing strategy that I've seen work very well is offering a "standard" and "premium" variation of a service or product. The "premium" version is priced at about 50% above the "standard" but offers twice or more value than the "standard" variation.

When using this strategy it's important to make sure that you are genuinely offering much more value with the "premium" than you are with the "standard." This strategy works extremely well in cases where the incremental cost of delivering the "premium" is relatively low, because the price differential ends up as pure profit on your bottom line.

Reverse Risk With "Unlimited"

Most people are extremely risk averse. They fear being stung by unexpected charges whether this be related to data usage, medical costs or consulting fees.

As we previously discussed, if you can remove this risk for them, you greatly increase the opportunity for a sale. An excellent strategy for removing this risk is to offer an "unlimited" variation of your product or service at a fixed price.

For example an IT company could offer "unlimited" technical support for a fixed monthly fee, a restaurant could offer "unlimited" beverage refills and so on. While many business owners fear that abuse of an unlimited option will send them broke, this can easily be remedied in your terms and conditions which would allow for fair use but would stop or limit abuse.

Especially when you are selling something that needs to be consumed in a particular time frame, the risk of offering an unlimited option is very low. Looking at your average transaction value over time and working with the law of averages can give you a very accurate idea of what it will cost you to offer an unlimited option.

People tend to overestimate how much they will use a product or service when they are at the point of purchase—my ab workout machine is a testament to this! So offering an unlimited option helps you capitalize on this as well as removing any perceived risk of overage charges.

The Ultra High Ticket Item

In every market there is a small percentage of the population who want to buy "the best" variant of a product in its class.

The indicator most often used by consumers as to what is "the best," is price. Some consumers will pay 10, 20 or 100 times the price of other functionally similar products e.g. Rolls Royce, private jet travel, etc.

While you might not sell these kinds of high ticket products every day of the week, if you don't make them available among your normal product mix, then you're definitely leaving money on the table.

These ultra high ticket items can make up a very large percentage of your net profit even if you only sell a small number of units. It will also help you attract a more affluent customer who shops based on prestige, service and convenience rather than on price.

Lastly, a big benefit of the ultra high ticket item is that it makes the other variations in your product range look much more reasonably priced by comparison. A rule of thumb often used is that ten percent of your customer base would pay ten times more and one percent of your customers would pay one hundred times more. Make sure you're not leaving money on the table by not having ultra high ticket items in your product mix.

Resist The Urge To Discount

When the market you operate in is highly competitive, there is a strong urge to discount your prices. This strategy needs to be used with extreme caution, because of the pressure it puts on your margins, profit and more importantly your market positioning.

Unless you have a very specific loss leader strategy, try to avoid discounting at all costs. With a loss leader strategy you try to entice a customer based on price and then upsell or cross sell other higher margin products or services.

A better option than discounting is to increase the value of your offering. Bundling in bonuses, increasing quantities or adding peripheral services can be of genuine value to your customer but cost you very little to do.

Regardless which specific strategies you implement, it is important to continually test and measure. Consumers are bags of emotion and are not driven purely by rational motivations.

Make the setting of price a central part of your overall marketing strategy.

Invite Them To Try Before They Buy

Some time ago I dropped into my local BMW dealership/service center to check out an error message I was getting on the car's computer system. A few minutes later the service clerk emerges after the garage had made a couple of small adjustments. "It's all sorted," he goes on to explain what the problem was with some technical car jargon. I nod my head knowingly, pretending to understand what he's saying to prevent the castration of my male ego.

Next he asks me, "Would you like to book the car in for a service? The car's computer indicates you're almost due." Nice upsell move. I say, "Sure let's book it in for mid next month." The service clerk then advises me that when making a booking that far in advance that I'm eligible for a loan vehicle for the day. I think great, that way I don't need to have anyone drop me off and pick me up. I request to borrow a car that is the next model up from mine.

This request should have sent their sales alarm bells ringing: existing customer with a three-year-old car that has just come out of warranty requesting to borrow and test drive the expensive next model up for a whole day. If ever a golden sales opportunity dropped in someone's lap, this was it. Instead of recognizing and grabbing this opportunity, he apologizes and says he can only give a loan of a car several models down from mine. Then he goes on for the next few minutes telling me how good this much cheaper model is.

I felt like knocking on his forehead and shouting "HELLO, anybody home, HELLO!" Or perhaps I should have channeled Julia Robert's character from *Pretty Woman* and said, "Big mistake. Huge. I have to go shopping now," and then stormed out. Instead I thanked him for his time and said, "I'll see you next month." I couldn't believe what had just transpired.

Did the service clerk really not see the opportunity? Unlikely. It was probably more of a case of "it's not my job." He probably thought something like, "Hey I'm in service, if he wants to test drive a new car, he should go see someone in sales." This is a mistake many businesses make. They segregate their staff into "departments." Therefore people outside of the sales department think that sales has nothing to do with them. Big mistake. Huge! As a business owner you should make it abundantly clear to all staff that sales are the lifeblood of the business and that **everyone is in sales**.

Every staff member at some stage will have the opportunity to positively or negatively influence a sales opportunity. Make it known that regardless of what their primary role in the business is, responding to sales opportunities **is their job**. One of the best ways to get this point across is to have an incentive program where sales get rewarded regardless of the position of the person they came from. You might even discover some hidden sales talent.

Of course the easiest sale to make is to an existing satisfied customer. Let all your staff know the cues to look out for—without being pushy or obnoxious of course.

Now granted, I may not have been ready to buy a new car right then and there, but would spending a full day with a car I've been eyeing off have gotten me closer to buying? Of course! Would it have started my buying juices flowing? Absolutely!

This brings us to another very powerful technique you can and should add to your follow-up sequence—try before you buy. Sometimes also known as a free trial or "the puppy dog close."

Picture the scenario—you're not sure if getting a new puppy is such a great idea, or perhaps you're unsure if this particular breed is the right fit. The pet store salesperson assures you that you can take the puppy home with you and if you don't like it, just bring it back—no questions asked. Sound reasonable? So you take the puppy home with you, you and the kids play fetch and run around outside with it. He licks your nose in the morning and waits for you faithfully at the door at the end of the day. So of course you all fall in love with the new member of the family. And the sale is made—not by the salesperson, but by the puppy.

It's that simple.

Try returning this little guy—I dare you

It's one of the most powerful ways to win more business and it's based on the magic of "try before you buy." Using this technique can dramatically boost your sales. First, it breaks down sales resistance, making the prospect feel less like their committing to something irreversible.

Second, it puts the onus on the buyer to reverse the sale which puts inertia back on your side. Lastly, a genuine customer is highly unlikely to return a good product that is meeting their needs. Implement the "everyone's in sales" mindset in your business and couple it with a "try before you buy" offer and you'll see dramatically better conversion results.

Close Down Your Sales Prevention Department

It never ceases to amaze me how many businesses, large and small, make it difficult to buy from them. It's almost like they have a sales prevention department, whose job is making the buying process a painful experience. Leave the red tape, lengthy forms and inflexible rules for government departments. Your job is to make it easy for customers to buy from you.

Signs that say "Cash Only" or "$10 Minimum For Credit Cards" or "We Don't Accept Amex" are the sales prevention department at work. These businesses may be saving money on merchant fees but are almost certainly losing far more in term of lost sales, lost customers and lost goodwill. They're stepping over dollars to pick up pennies.

You need to offer your customers **their** preferred payment method—not yours. Also don't punish customers for using their preferred payment method by adding a surcharge. Rather factor merchant fees into your general pricing or absorb them. If your competition is intense or your margins are so thin that you can't afford to factor merchant fees into your general pricing then you have some far bigger problems to solve than just merchant fees.

As mentioned in Chapter 2, another strategy for increasing your conversions is to offer a payment plan or finance for your higher ticket items. This can mean the difference between a sale and no sale. First, people often think of both their income and expenses on a monthly basis. Second, people are far less attached to future money than present money. Present money is usually already spent. If you can present your offer in easy bite-sized monthly chunks or a future obligation, rather than a big lump sum, this will dramatically increase conversions.

Look for other things that could be roadblocks to sales conversion. Are you requiring prospects and customers to jump through hoops, fill in useless forms or conform to processes that aren't really necessary? How could you remove these roadblocks or at the very least make them much easier?

ACT III

The "After" Phase

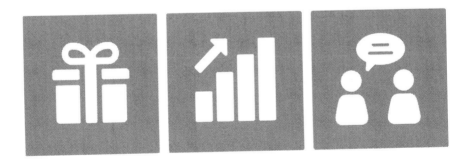

The "After" Phase Section Summary

In the "after" phase you're dealing with customers. Customers are people that like you and what you have to offer enough to have paid you money at least once. In this phase you'll turn your customers into raving fans by delivering a world class experience. You'll then find ways of doing more business with them and increasing their lifetime value. Finally you'll create an environment where referrals continually come your way.

The goal of this final phase is to get your customers to trust you and buy more from you. This phase continues in an ongoing "virtuous cycle" where you deepen your relationship with customers, do more business with them and get more referrals.

Chapter 7

Delivering A World Class Experience

Chapter 7 Summary

By delivering a world class experience, you turn customers into a tribe of raving fans who want to buy from you repeatedly. To deliver this world class experience you need to implement systems in your business and make smart use of technology.

Highlights covered in this chapter include:

- Why building a tribe of raving fans is crucial to your business success and how to do it.
- The two critical functions of your business.
- How to innovate even when the product or service you sell is boring and ordinary.
- The purpose of technology in your business and how to leverage this in your marketing,
- Why systems are the key to uncovering a fortune that lies hidden in your business.
- The four main systems in your business that virtually guarantee your business success.
- How to eliminate the biggest bottleneck in your business.

Building Your Tribe Of Raving Fans

A tribe is a group of people connected to one another, connected to a leader and connected to an idea[9]. For thousands of years, human beings have been part of one tribe or another.

One of the things that separates extraordinary businesses from ordinary ones is that they lead tribes, tribes of raving fans—not just customers. In your business, a tribe member is a special type of customer. One that acts as a cheerleader and is actively conspiring for you success. Your tribe members amplify your marketing message and take it to heights you'd never be able to reach on your own with paid advertising. Here are a few of the qualities of these extraordinary businesses that become tribe leaders:

- They continually focus on wowing their customers which turns them into raving fans
- They create and foster lifetime relationships
- They make it easy and fun to deal with them
- They create a sense of theatre around their products and services
- They have systems so that they can reliably and consistently deliver a great experience

In this chapter we're going to look at some strategies for turning customers into raving fans who trust you, refer you and can't wait to do more business with you. These people are your tribe and it's vital to have strategies for building such a following and taking great care of them.

Most ordinary businesses stop their marketing efforts once they've converted a prospect into a customer (i.e., the prospect buys from them). This sort of transactional thinking keeps them stuck and puts a firm lid on their business growth. By contrast truly remarkable businesses get exponential results because each customer they add is not just revenue once but it's revenue over and over again because this person becomes an evangelist for your business.

Even more exciting than that, new product launches become easy and predictable. You don't have to market, hustle and convince as much

---

[9]   This definition was taken from Seth Godin's excellent book *Tribes*.

when you have a tribe of raving fans. Look at Apple, one of the leaders in this type of marketing. They can launch a brand new product or even a new category of product and they already have a legion of raving fans queuing up days in advance begging Apple to take their money. This is isn't just the domain of large companies like Apple.

In fact it's an area where small businesses have a massive advantage. Unlike large businesses that are inflexible and steeped in bureaucracy, have numerous lines of reporting and people with varying agendas, small businesses can be agile and respond to customer needs and feedback quickly. More importantly, small businesses can micromanage the customer relationship. The customer doesn't as easily get lost in a sea of other customers and a relationship can be developed which is much more personal and much more tribe like. It's your job to create and foster a tribe of raving fans and understand that the marketing process really only just begins once you convert a prospect into a paying customer.

Sell Them What They Want But Give Them What They Need

In Chapter 2 we talked about the essential elements of crafting a good offer. As discussed in that chapter, the first step in crafting a good offer is to find out exactly what your market wants. Now I want to go deeper. When it comes to delivery of your product or service we need to give our customers not just what they want but what they need.

There's often a big difference between what people want and what people need. Let me give you an example. Let's say you're a fitness instructor. You improve people's lives through better health, fitness and nutrition. The concept of better health is too vague, far off and long-term for most people. So instead you've got to appeal to vanity, performance or some other specific want that the prospect has—for example ripped abs, toned body, great figure.

So you need to give them what they need in terms of health improvement but do it via what they want and that's what you sell them, which was the improvements in appearance and performance. You need to understand both wants and needs. They are sometimes overlapping and sometimes completely non-overlapping.

If I've owned a treadmill for a long time but I haven't lost any weight, does this prove that treadmills don't work? This is obviously a ridiculous conclusion. For my treadmill to "work" I've obviously got to turn it on, run on it for a while, sweat and repeat the process on a regular basis. Buying it is just the first step. Putting it to its intended use is another. While this may seem obvious, a big part of the battle you'll fight is getting people to do what they need to do to achieve results with your product or service.

Some business owners feel like following through to implementation is not their responsibility. That their customer should be responsible for getting results with the product or service they have bought. However, this is short-sighted. We live in a world that's fast paced with a lot of things competing for the time and attention of our customers. Our goal is for our customers to achieve results.

A customer who buys a product or service and doesn't use it or implement it correctly is highly likely to write it off as something that doesn't work and that's the last thing we want. At best it ends up being a one-off sale and at worst it ends up being labeled a scam. As ridiculous as someone calling treadmills a scam because they failed to actually use it, a consumer can do the same with your product or service.

Except now the consumer has access to online forums and social media and will either spread positive feedback if they got positive results or negative feedback if they didn't. Unfair? Maybe—but the mark of winning businesses is going to be turn-key solutions that help customers through implementation to the desired result.

In many cases it's going to mean you need to spoon feed them through the process of getting results. Otherwise you're in a low margin, commodity, transaction style business competing solely on price and that's a dangerous place to be with price comparisons being only a click away.

So your job is now to find a way to sell what your prospects want but also give them what they need. To get them to take action and do what they need to do to get results may mean that you have to package things in a certain way. You may need to cut the process up into manageable bite-sized pieces so that it doesn't seem so daunting.

You may have the best vitamin in the world, but you need to make it taste sweet so the kids will eat it. That's giving them what they want but also what they need.

Leadership is an attractive quality and people want to be led. By taking the initiative of packaging up the implementation of your product or service, anticipating roadblocks that will be encountered along the way and having solutions to overcoming these roadblocks shows leadership. Helping your customers all the way through to achieving results will have a big payoff for both yourself and them.

Not doing so will short change the both of you. Remember your goal is to create a tribe of raving fans—not just transactions.

Create Theatre Around Your Products and Services

Peter Drucker is famously quoted as saying that the two basic functions of every business are marketing and innovation. The word innovation often conjures up thoughts of high tech startups in Silicon Valley, biotech companies or engineering firms. The question often arises—can an ordinary business that sells ordinary products be innovative? The answer is of course yes.

A common misconception is that the innovation has to be in the actual product or service itself. If you sell a boring or ordinary product it may seem like innovation may not be relevant to your business or industry. It may seem you have no option but to compete solely on price.

However, innovation can go far beyond the actual product that's sold. Innovation can be applied to how the product is priced, financed, packaged, supported, delivered, managed, marketed or a myriad of other elements related to any part of the customer experience. One area where businesses fail spectacularly is creating a sense of theatre. Your customers don't just want to be serviced. They want to be entertained. Give them what they want by creating a sense of theatre around your product.

If you're in an "unsexy" business where your customer's first question is generally centered around price, you may be a bit skeptical about all this talk of innovation and theatre. After all how can a manufacturer of blenders really be innovative? Or perhaps a restaurant? How can these ordinary, boring businesses be innovative? I'm glad you asked.

Blendtec is a manufacturer of blenders—ordinary blenders like the type you would use in your kitchen at home. They've created an enormous viral marketing buzz by making a YouTube video series called "Will It Blend"? Here they have a whacky looking scientist demonstrate their product by blending a variety of weird objects from iPhones and iPads to golf balls.

To see the Blendtec video series visit 1pmp.com

I want to cry after seeing the wanton destruction of my favorite Apple products; however, Blendtec must be pretty happy about the hundreds of millions of views on their YouTube channel. That kind of publicity compared to the small cost involved in producing these videos is just genius. Could you similarly create a sense of theatre and publicity by demonstrating your ordinary product being used in unusual ways?

I was in the men's room at a local restaurant in my area when I noticed this poster on the wall:

The restaurant offers a pick up and drop off service so customers don't have to worry about driving under the influence. It creates convenience for the customer and the restaurant ends up selling more of their highest margin product—alcohol. Everyone wins.

These are just a couple of examples of ordinary, otherwise boring businesses that are selling their products in innovative ways. Now it's time for you to innovate. You don't have to invent anything original. Model, borrow or shamelessly steal innovative ideas from other industries or products.

Do anything other than stay a boring commodity which forces you to compete solely on price.

Use Technology To Reduce Friction

My wife and I were recently dining at one of our favorite restaurants. The food there is great, the staff are courteous and helpful and the location is spectacular—right on the beach. On a cold night they have a log wood fireplace going which really adds to the atmosphere. We've been dining there for about a year or so—ever since we moved to the area. As I went to pay for the meal, I looked over and sure enough it was still there—a tattered hand-written sign near their credit card machine that says, "Sorry our credit card machine doesn't work with PINs, please sign instead. Apologies for the inconvenience."

I marveled at how such a high-end restaurant that has got so much right, has got this one fundamental thing wrong. As a business owner, if there's one part of interacting with my customers that I want to be as smooth and frictionless as possible, it's the part where I get paid. Not only was this faulty credit card machine not attended to for at least a year (that I know of) but they clearly had no intention of implementing new, even more frictionless payment technology such as contactless.

The rate of technology innovation over the past few years has been nothing short of astonishing. Prior to August 2004 Google was still a private, relatively unknown company. Prior to September 2006 Facebook was still just an experiment and not yet open to the public.

In mid-2007 there was no iPhone and in April 2010 the iPad was still just a rumor in geek circles. We almost can't imagine life without some of these technologies—yet a few short years ago they didn't even exist. While the pace of technology innovation has increased and continues to increase exponentially, the purpose of new technology has remained constant over thousands of years.

Plain and simple **the purpose of any new technology in your business is to eliminate friction.** We want the fastest and easiest path to the sale, while increasing customer satisfaction. We also want to avoid situations where technology hinders rather than facilitates business:

As customers (of usually large institutions) we've all had the frustrating experience of trying to talk sense to someone who's being held back by technology and responds with their version of "Computer says 'No'...." As small business owners we must ensure technology is being used in our businesses in ways that remove friction rather than creating it.

Technology makes our lives easier by doing the "heavy lifting" on our behalf, whether it's doing a complex calculation, lifting a concrete block into place or searching through thousands of publications to find that obscure literary reference you're looking for. Yet sometimes it's like we implement technology for technology's sake. For example I often ask people what the purpose of their website, Twitter or Facebook page is. I rarely get a succinct and direct answer.

Back when the iPod came out, this was the only legal way to load new music onto it:

- Drive down to the local music store and buy a CD with the music you want.
- Insert the CD into the computer and import the contents into your computer hard drive.
- Sync the iPod with the computer so it copies all the music over.

Despite this painful process, the iPod was still a huge success; however, when Apple introduced the iTunes Store, the success of the iPod exploded and it also laid the foundation for the iPhone and iPad. The technology Apple introduced greatly reduced the friction between consumer and merchant. The same can be said of Amazon, Google, contactless payment technologies and much more.

By reducing friction, technology helps us do in a fraction of the time what would have taken us hours, days or years to accomplish without it. So how can you use technology to reduce the friction between you and your customers? What tasks can you streamline and make seamless? More importantly how can you ensure technology isn't hindering your relationship with your customers? Here's how I do it.

Think of each piece of technology as an employee. What am I hiring this employee to do? What are its key performance indicators (KPIs)? Take the example of a website. It's pretty common that a business will have a website with no specific goal—just some vague notion or hope that customers will come their way because they have put up an online version of their brochure.

By contrast, every smart entrepreneur I know uses technology with very specific goals in mind that are measurable. For example a website can be used for selling a product or getting prospects to opt-in to a marketing database. These things are measurable and can have KPI's attached to them. We know instantly if they're working or not and we fire the ones that aren't working and we continue improving the ones that are.

Now may be a good time to rethink the various ways you use technology in your business. Are they reducing friction? Are they doing what they were hired to do?

Become A Voice Of Value To Your Tribe

The late great Jim Rohn said it well:

> *"Don't spend most of your time on the voices that don't count. Tune out the shallow voices so that you will have more time to tune in the valuable ones."*

It's certainly wise advice; however, part of delivering a world class experience to your customers is **becoming** a voice of value to them. You need to be a thought leader in your industry. Someone who is sought out for opinion and comment. You do this by becoming a creator of content. One of the major distinctions between successful entrepreneurs and "wantrepreneurs" is that successful entrepreneurs are predominantly content creators whereas wantrepreneurs are predominantly content consumers. Even more than just content creators, successful entrepreneurs are often **prolific** content creators.

To become a voice of value, you need to have valuable ideas and rarely do valuable ideas come from nowhere and interrupt you. By seeking out other voices of value—thought leaders in and out of your industry, mentors, coaches and successful peers, you lay the foundation for building your own valuable ideas.

This type of self-education is the most valuable type of education I know of. Yet it's important not to let too many voices in, however tempting that may be. A few voices who speak from experience and firsthand knowledge are infinitely more valuable than a multitude of voices that speak from theory and opinion. While neither theory nor opinion are bad in themselves, rarely do I find voices of value from sources that haven't been where I want to be.

The days of high pressure selling tactics are fast coming to an end, if they haven't already. In an age where everyone is connected and everyone has access to almost all the available information, the most valuable commodity is reputation. The reputation economy requires that you transform your marketing from just information and high pressure sales tactics to education-based marketing. As we've discussed throughout this book, the point of education marketing is twofold.

Firstly, it's about positioning yourself as an authority in your target market. Everyone wants to hear from an authoritative source. By being a content creator, you position yourself as an authority and expert in your niche.

Secondly, it's about building relationships—becoming the trusted advisor to your target market rather than just a salesperson. By regularly releasing valuable, educational content to your target market, you lay the foundation for a relationship—and after all who would you prefer to buy from, a trusted source who has been giving you a lot of value or a stranger who wants to make a quick sale?

Becoming a voice of value is hard work and it takes time, but the time invested will pay dividends. In the reputation economy you can't afford to be a commodity or another "me too" type of business. What can you do to start being a voice of value in your market? Could you start a blog? A mailing list? A monthly newsletter? Regular YouTube videos?

Any one of these things could be the start of you becoming a voice of value to your market place. Certainly doing so will set you far apart from your competitors who are still stuck on the selling tactics that are no longer working.

Tell Them All The Trouble You Go To

My wife and I were driving home one night after a being out to dinner and I was looking forward to a nice relaxing end to my Saturday night when I heard those dreaded words, "Let's stop off at the supermarket, I just need to pick up a couple of things." I groaned and pulled into the parking lot. Hating shopping more than almost anything else I tried my old classic line, "I'll wait for you in the car"—after all she was only picking up a couple of things and I could use that time productively on my iPhone to catapult some angry birds and complete that level I've been stuck on. But she'd have none of it. I finally found myself in the last aisle of the supermarket, holding a shopping basket heavy with the broken promise of "just a couple of things." While my wife was busy deciding between grapefruit or coconut shampoo (that's a marketing lesson in itself), something caught my eye—a brilliant marketing ninja move, perfectly executed. See the picture I took of it below:

Can you see the huge difference between the two bottles of shower gel on the right versus the one on the left? The two bottles on the right are one of the best uses of product packaging I've seen in a long time. The one on the left is boring, safe and almost indistinguishable from the one hundred others on the shelf.

It takes a long time to pour a full glass of Guinness. This is because of a process called nucleation in which pockets of air from additional bubbles diffuse through the beer. While this is now appreciated, originally there was a lot of negative consumer opinion about the length of time required to correctly pour a pint of Guinness from the tap. During the mid-1990s Guinness turned all this around with a marketing campaign that sold this negative attribute as a positive feature. They started essentially telling the people how much effort went into pouring the perfect beer. They emphasized this by saying "it takes 119.5 seconds to pour the perfect pint" and "good things come to those who wait."

Here's the lesson—**tell your audience about all the effort that goes into delivering your product or service.** In your sales copy and even in your packaging give them the details of how you painstakingly prepare or manufacture your product. This applies equally if you deliver services. Tell them about your skills, how you acquired them, all the checks and balances you have in place and how you train your staff. The backstory to your product or service is an absolutely essential part of your marketing. Don't let your efforts and skill go unnoticed. It gives them an assurance that there is substance and quality behind your product. This is especially important if you are pitching a premium product or service.

Looking back at my photo of the shower gel above, you can see that the backstory here takes up the entire space on the bottle. There isn't even a logo or company name—very smart and very good use of prime real estate! The fact is, **no one cares about your logo, company name or some dubious claim about being the leader in your industry.** They want to know about what your product will do for them, and your backstory is essential to this.

So there you have it, I went from being an unwilling participant in a shopping trip to seeing a new twist on a valuable marketing principle—good things indeed come to those who wait.

Products Make You Money, Systems Make You A Fortune

One of the major things I have always concentrated on in all my businesses is creating systems. After first reading Michael Gerber's book *The E-Myth*, I was hooked. The penny dropped inside the business part of my brain. Good thing too because I've done very well out of business systems. In fact, this is one thing that took me from struggling and broke in business to doing well and able to successfully exit multiple startups.

The most valuable business systems are those which are replicable. If your business relies on a genius or superstar talent at the center of it, then it's difficult or impossible to replicate. That's one of the reasons inventor Warren Buffet only invests in "boring businesses"—ones he can understand, that deliver a staple product, that have solid management and generate a lot of cash—how boring!

Among his portfolio you won't see any high risk technology startups, highly speculative biotech companies or concepts you can't understand.

These often rely on one or two superstars that would kill the company should they leave. Instead you'll see solid businesses that have systems which deliver excellent products consistently over a long period of time. **Systems allow mere mortals to run an extraordinary business.**

Once you have a business system that is replicable, people will want to pay you large sums of money for it. This will come in many forms but the most common are:

- Customers wanting to do business with you because you deliver consistent results
- Licensees wanting to license your system
- Franchisees who want to buy into your franchise system
- An investor or competitor wanting to buy out your business

There are four main types of business systems you need to create regardless of what type of business you're in. You're almost guaranteed to make a fortune if you can create scalable and replicable systems in these four areas of your business:

Marketing system – Generate a consistent flow of leads into the business.

Sales system – Lead nurturing, follow-up and conversion.

Fulfillment system – The actual thing you do in exchange for the customer's money.

Administration system – Accounts, reception, human resources, etc. Support of all the other business functions.

Regardless of what business you run, these four functions will be relevant to you.

Many small businesses get bogged down with fulfillment and administration while neglecting their marketing and sales systems. After all, no one is pressuring you with deadlines to get you to do more marketing. All the seemingly urgent issues generally fall into the fulfillment and administration functions. This causes the common situation where the business is struggling, even though they might be offering excellent products and services.

The problem is that **customers don't find out how good your products and services are until they have bought from you**. And if your marketing and sales systems aren't in place, they will never buy in the first place and find out how good you are. It's a vicious cycle.

Some rely on reputation and word of mouth. While these are great, it takes a very long time to build up enough business purely on reputation. Smart businesses on the other hand go to great lengths to perfect their marketing and sales systems. After all there's very few business problems that can't be solved with money.

So what exactly is a business system?

In short, business systems start with documented procedures and processes that allow your business to run without you. Most often this is in the form of checklists but video and audio training can also be an important part of it. Collectively these materials are referred to as an **operations manual** and its purpose is to capture the collective "know how" of the business.

The poster child for business systems is McDonald's. This is a complex, worldwide, multi-billion dollar business that is essentially run by pimply teenagers who can't even be trusted to make their beds. How do they do this? They have amazing business systems. Their operations manual covers every minute detail of the business from big things like hiring and customer interaction to knowing exactly how much sauce to squeeze onto a Big Mac bun and how many pickles should be on it. I should know. As a teenager, I used to work there. Here's a little something I found when I was moving house a few years ago.

In my experience there are two major reasons why business systems are overlooked by many small business owners.

The first reason is because business systems are "back office" functions. Unlike the latest product offering, sales techniques or other highly visible aspects of your business, good business systems are considered by some as boring. While building them may indeed be boring, the incredible power they give you is anything but.

The second major reason that business systems are neglected is because of a perceived lack of urgency. When a business is small or just starting out, there are seemingly much more important things to do like sales, administration and order fulfillment. With all of these important things vying for the increasingly scarce time of the business owner, business systems seem like something that can be put off until later. However, just like any other accumulation of neglect over time, it rarely ends well.

It's a sad situation when a business owner goes to sell their business and finds out after putting in many years of hard work, that their business is worthless. It's not so much that the business itself is worthless, it's that they ARE the business and without them there is no real business to sell. In cases like this they can't sell it for any kind of reasonable sum beyond the value of their stock and maybe a small, nominal amount for "good will."

There are numerous benefits to implementing systems in your business. Here are some of the most important.

It builds a valuable asset. It's nice if your business gives you a great cash flow to fund your lifestyle. But wouldn't it be fabulous if one day when you decided it was time, you could sell your business and have the biggest pay day of your life? You can only do this if you build the value of the business and that can only happen if it is a system that can continue running without you.

Leverage and scalability. Systems give your business the ability to expand. You can replicate your business in other geographic areas yourself or by franchising or licensing the rights to your business system. Many fortunes have been made this way.

Consistency. Consistency is one of the keys to delivering an excellent customer experience. You may not like the food at McDonald's but one thing you can say about them is that wherever you go they deliver a very consistent experience.

Lower labor costs. When you and your staff don't have to waste time and effort re-inventing the wheel each time, this improves your efficiency and reduces your labor costs.

The Power Of Systems—The Ability To Fire Yourself

Let me ask you a question. If you went overseas for six months leaving your business behind, when you came back would it be in better or worse shape than you left it? Would you even have a business left to come back to? If you answered in the negative to either of these questions, then it's likely you don't have a business—rather you ARE the business. Many small businesses, especially when they are sole operators or where all the partners work in the business, make the mistake for reasons outlined above, of not thinking about systems. After all the business is small and the founder or founders perform all roles. Unfortunately this thought processes dooms them to staying small and remaining a prisoner in their business.

They often find themselves in a catch-22 situation. They have no time to work on the business because they are too busy working in the business. And they can't get away from the business because they haven't developed documented systems and processes. So they're stuck in a business that has become a self-made prison. Don't get me wrong, they may be financially successful. Their business may be thriving with a loyal base of customers but the problem is they are stuck—shackled to their business.

If they were to leave or get sick for an extended period of time, their business would cease to exist. The problem is that all the "know how" of the business is stuck in a silo between their ears. The only way out is to make time to create and document these business systems. Thankfully this daunting process is not that difficult when we break it into chunks.

Our goal is to eliminate the biggest bottleneck from your business—YOU. Even if you're not looking to get out of your business immediately, the day will come when you need to take time off, want to go onto another venture, employ more staff or even sell your business. When the time comes you'll be thankful you followed this advice.

Your job as an entrepreneur is to be an innovator and a builder of systems. Even if you are a sole operator right now, it's important to think long-term and think big. The first part of the process is to think of your business as being ten times the size it currently is. If that were the case what roles would exist? For example, would you have someone taking care of the bookkeeping, someone else in shipping, another person in sales, a marketing person, etc.? You get the idea.

If you're a sole operator or a small business, it's not a problem if you currently perform all or most of the roles in your business. But it is a problem if you currently **have to** perform all the roles in your business. If you are indispensable, you are a bottleneck and the business will only move as fast as you can.

We need to start looking at each role in the business. Now when I say role I don't mean person. For example, in a small business the same person might be both on reception and doing the bookkeeping. Now even though one person does both of these roles they are still two separate roles and if the business were larger these two roles would be performed by different people. In an even larger business a single role might be broken up even further. For example, there might be a separate bookkeeper for accounts payable and accounts receivable. Once you've identified all the different roles in your business, you can start defining what tasks each role performs. For example what are all the tasks we expect the person performing the bookkeeping role to do? These tasks may include:

- Invoicing customers
- Bank reconciliation
- Following up unpaid invoices
- Entering supplier invoices
- Etc.

Now once we've identified all the roles within the business and defined what tasks each role does, we now need to document exactly how each task should be performed.

One of the best tools you can use in building business systems is checklists. Checklists are easy to create, follow and track. Once you've created a list of all the tasks performed in your business, you are ready to start documenting exactly how these tasks are performed.

A simplified example for the task "Following up unpaid invoices" could look something like:

- Run accounts receivable report
- For any invoices that are 7-13 days overdue send a friendly reminder
- For any invoices that are 14-27 days overdue call the customer to remind them to pay
- Forward any invoices that are more than 27 days overdue to our debt collection agency

See how we've broken the task down into small easy-to-follow steps? Now granted the above is a simplistic example for illustration purposes. In fact some of these steps include subtasks which would also need to be documented—for example how do you run an accounts receivable report?

So to recap—it's essentially a three step process:

1. Identify all of the roles in your business
2. Define what tasks each role performs
3. Create checklists for properly completing these tasks

Now if you wanted to delegate or outsource a task, it's going to be so much easier to hand the person a step-by-step process rather than just giving them ad hoc training and watching over them constantly to make sure they do it right.

Now scaling your business becomes super easy—just add people. Once you see the awesome power of systems in your business you'll never go back to the old way of doing things.

As you can see, this process is a way of getting the processes you already have in place documented. Currently all these processes may be stored in your head and accessible only to you. Documenting these business systems will be the only way to easily scale your business and let it run without you.

Importantly this also ensures that your customers get a consistent experience. If, or rather when, staff join or leave your business you want to ensure that customers still get the same, world class experience. You can't leave this to the discretion of individual staff. It has to come from the business and having documented systems is by far the best way I know of doing this.

Your Ultimate Customer

Neil Armstrong once said, *"You only have to solve two problems when going to the moon: first, how to get there; and second, how to get back. The key is don't leave until you have solved both problems."*

In the excitement of starting a business, it's common to spend a lot of time thinking about "how to get there," that is become successful, but often what's given less thought is "how to get back"—i.e. the exit strategy.

When starting a business it's important to think clearly and plan for how you will exit. This sounds obvious but is something many business owners don't think about until it's too late. How's it going to end? Who will your buyer be? Why will they buy your business? Will they buy you out for your customer base, for the revenue, for the intellectual property? How will they get a return on their investment? Answering some of these questions will help you visualize exactly who your buyer is and why they would buy you. It's crucial to think about these things at the beginning because they will help you shape exactly how you engineer your business and what you focus on. If your goal is to exit a business for $50 million then everything you do in your business can be framed with the question—will this help me get $50 million?

You'll rarely make as much money running a business as you will selling one. The person or company who puts you out of business is your ultimate customer and satisfying them will result in the biggest pay day you'll ever receive. Countless fortunes have been made this way. Sadly a very large number of businesses are worthless and eventually just get wound down because the owner wants to or has to move on and has not been able to secure a buyer. This is why it's so crucial to structure things in a way that ensures you're on the receiving end of a big pay day rather than faced with the realization that your years of hard work have come to naught as far as the value of the business is concerned.

Over the years I've sold multiple businesses and now as an angel investor, I'm on the other side of the table—evaluating businesses I feel would be worth buying into. I can tell you one of the most important things a purchaser looks for and that you need to satisfy is whether you HAVE a business or whether you ARE the business. There's an enormous difference. If your business can't be operated without you, then it's not a saleable asset and you're stuck—regardless of how good or profitable it is. That's why business systems are so crucial. Having documented systems is what enables the business to run without you.

Next you need to consider who will buy your business and why. Will it be a competitor? Someone new to the industry? Someone in your industry but in a different niche? Structuring the business with a logical acquirer in mind is smart and it's something that's very attractive to investors. It shows them a clear path to exit and return of their invested capital. Even if you don't plan to take on investors, as the owner of the business, you should think of yourself as an investor. You wear the entrepreneur hat by day but at night the investor hat should come on and you should be questioning when that return on invested capital is going to occur and how.

One of the most common objections I hear from owner-operators is, "I love what I'm doing and I don't intend to sell." That's great if what you love doing is making you a good income—relatively few people enjoy such a lifestyle. But whether you like it or not, one day your circumstances will change. You may get bored, get sick, want to retire, see a better opportunity, etc.

When, not if, that time comes and you do decide it's time to sell, you want to be able to walk away with a check that has a lot of zeros on it rather than have to wind it all down and possibly end up in debt or sell for a pittance. If you start thinking about structuring for exit at the time you need to exit, you're toast. It's way too late and you're very unlikely to achieve a favorable result. You need to start with the end in mind. Start thinking about your ultimate customer and what would motivate them to write you that check which becomes your biggest pay day.

> ### Chapter 7 Action Item:
> ### How Will You Deliver A World Class Experience?
> ### Fill in square #7 of your 1-Page Marketing Plan

Chapter 8

Increasing Customer Lifetime Value

Chapter 8 Summary

Increasing the lifetime value of existing customers is where the real money is made. To do this you need to have strategies and tactics for getting existing customers to do more business with you. You also need to know, manage and continually improve key numbers in your business.

Highlights covered in this chapter include:

- Why your existing customer base is a rich diamond mine and how to realize its value.
- Five major ways to make more money from existing customers.
- How to win back lost customers or reactivate customers that haven't bought from you recently.
- The critical marketing metrics you must know and manage.
- An example where slightly improving three key numbers generated a 431% improvement to the bottom line.
- Why not all business growth and revenue is good and how to avoid "polluted revenue".
- The four categories of customers in your business and why you shouldn't treat them equally.

Acres Of Diamonds

As entrepreneurs we're often focused on the kill. We're closers, hustlers and we like the taste of fresh blood in our mouths. That's the sexy stuff which we discussed in detail in the first six chapters of this book. It's the "front end" offer which brings the new customer through the door.

In this chapter I want to focus on the "back end." That's the stuff that makes your existing customers buy more. I know this isn't as sexy as discussing positioning, closing techniques or cool marketing strategies to get new customers but trust me this chapter is where the real money is made.

Russell Conwell's classic speech "Acres of Diamonds" is about a man, Ali Hafed, who wanted to find diamonds so badly that he sold his farm, left his family and went off on a search that took him all over the world. His search was futile and ultimately led to nothing but his own demise. Meanwhile the new owner of his farm discovers "the most magnificent diamond mine in all the history of mankind" right there on the farm that he had purchased from Ali Hafed.

> **To hear an audio of the "Acres Of Diamonds" speech or read a transcript visit 1pmp.com**

The moral of the story being "dig first on your own property when seeking treasure." I think this applies perfectly to marketing. Most businesses have a rich "diamond mine" in the form of existing customers which remains largely untapped, yet they leave this "family" of existing customers after the first few transactions and spend all their marketing energy, money and resources on seeking new sources of revenue.

While much of this book rightly focuses on getting new customers, which is vital, that's only one of the two ways to grow your business. The other way is to make more from existing and past customers. Most businesses, especially if they've been around for a while, are sitting on a veritable diamond mine. Increasing revenue and more importantly profit from existing and past customers is far easier than getting new ones. A widely quoted statistic[10] is that a person is 21 times more likely to buy from a business whom they've bought from in the past compared to one they've never purchased from. That puts you at a huge selling advantage when it comes to your current and past customers. The real profit is in figuring out how to sell more to existing and past customers and increasing their lifetime value. Let's look at five major ways to do this.

Raising Prices

One of the most overlooked ways of increasing the lifetime value of a customer is simply by raising prices. Most business fear that raising prices could lead to a customer exodus or backlash of some sort. While it does need to be handled strategically, you'll generally find your customers are far less price sensitive than you imagine. Especially if you're positioning yourself correctly as discussed in Chapter 6 and delivering a great customer experience as discussed in the previous chapter then most customers will happily accept them and depending on how you transact with your customers, some may not even notice.

Reverse roles for a moment and think back to your own purchasing habits, how often have you caught yourself just swiping your credit card without even looking at the total, let alone itemizing the whole bill? Personally, I find this is very often the case, especially when it comes to lower value goods and services. Even though I visit my local cafe often, I don't know exactly what they charge for a coffee. Even more importantly if they raised their prices by ten or twenty percent I'd likely be none the wiser. I just tap my card and wait for it to be served. For the owner of the cafe though, I suspect a ten or twenty percent increase on the bottom

---

[10] This statistic has been bandied about for years. I'm not even going to attempt to try to track it down to it's original source. In reality whether the number is actually 21, 18, 5 or whatever is pretty irrelevant. What is relevant is that it is orders of magnitude easier to sell to people who've previously purchased from you than it is to try and sell to new prospects.

line would be significant—possibly the difference between struggling and thriving.

When was the last time you actually increased your prices? If it's been a while then it may be time to reassess. Here's the thing—if you hold your prices constant for a long time, in real terms you're effectively lowering them because inflation makes the same nominal amount of money less valuable over time. Inflation is the sustained increase in the general price level of goods and services over a period of time. Think about the price of milk or bread when you were kid compared to now? That's inflation at work. By not increasing your prices over a long period of time you're effectively giving yourself a pay cut.

The key to raising your prices in a way that makes it palatable to your clients is giving them a reason why. Explain to them the increases in quality of your product or the increased input costs that you've borne. Explain to them the benefits they've already received from your offering and how they'll benefit from your future innovations. Some percentage of customers may leave you despite your explanation; however, they tend to be the lowest value customers. A customer won on price will be lost on price. If it's done right, the increase in profit gained by raising your prices will outweigh any lost revenue from price sensitive churners.

If you're particularly concerned that your existing customers won't tolerate a price increase, you can try "grandfathering." This is where the price increase is only applicable to new customers and existing ones are "grandfathered" in at the current price level. If you do this, ensure you tell your existing customers what you're doing as this can reinforce to them what a great deal they're getting and increase their loyalty to you since you're making them feel special.

Upselling

"Would you like fries with that?" is responsible for hundreds of millions of dollars to McDonald's and a similar upsell strategy could be worth a fortune to you. Upselling is the bundling of add-ons with the primary product or service being sold.

In Robert Cialdini's classic book *Influence: The Psychology of Persuasion*, he discusses the contrast principle. The contrast principle comes into play when two different things presented sequentially feel more different than they really are. For example if you lift a heavy object first followed by a light one, you'll judge the second object to be lighter than it really is. If your neighbor is having a really loud party all evening, the peace and quiet you suddenly appreciate more when it's over is the contrast principle in effect.

The exact same thing applies to price. When prospects buy the primary "expensive" item first, the suggested add-ons feel comparatively cheap. Men who've shopped for a suit will know exactly what I mean. You get to the counter with the suit you've picked out expecting to pay the price on the tag. In reality, your shopping journey is just beginning. The sales clerk now starts discussing your shirt requirements. Normally you might have balked at such expensive shirts but in contrast to the price of the suit, the shirts seem reasonably priced. Five shirts later, the sales assistant is complimenting your excellent taste in shirts and helping color match ties to go with them. When you finally think it's over, out come the socks and belts. When all's said and done your transaction value has possibly doubled or tripled.

Two things work in your favor with upsells. First, the contrast principle as already discussed. Second, because the prospect was not specifically shopping for your suggested add-ons they're much less likely to be price sensitive to the item being attached. Both of these factors mean much higher margins for you. While I don't recommend it as a strategy, it's not uncommon for the primary product to have thin margins with the real profit being in the upsells. Consumer electronics are often sold that way with razor thin margin on the core products and most of the real profit coming from add on accessories like cables, batteries and the extended warranties.

A great way of framing an upsell is, "most customers who bought X also bought Y." You see this done well in large ecommerce stores like Amazon. People want to participate in social norms. By telling them what "normal" buying habits are, you tap into the powerful, deep-seated psychological human desire to fit in.

Some mistakenly think that when a customer has just bought, they need to be given a break before attempting to sell to them again. Nothing could be further from the truth. When the prospect is "hot and heavy" and in the buying state of mind, they'll be much more receptive to other offers to buy. This is your opportunity to bundle in a high margin add on. It gives the customer a better result and instantly increases your customer lifetime value.

Ascension

Ascension is the process of moving existing customers to your higher priced, and hopefully higher margin, products and services. It's the ISP selling you the higher speed Internet plan or the car dealer selling you the next model up. Ascension campaigns should be a constant part of your marketing process. Very often customers stay on existing products or services even though they can benefit from and afford to move up. This is inertia working against you.

Other than just making you more profit, ascension campaigns help you combat inertia and can prevent customers from switching to a competitor. When customers independently consider moving up because your current product or service is no longer meeting their needs, they will often look at what your competitors have to offer and blame you for the poor experience they're having with your product or service. All they see is the Internet service you sold them is frustratingly slow or the car you sold has terrible fuel economy. It may well be their fault for choosing that cheap option three years ago but it's your fault and your problem if you lose them because you weren't proactive enough to keep up with their needs.

Equally bad is only one pricing option or only one option for each product or service category. Having only one option means that you're leaving huge sums of money on the table. At minimum you need to have a "standard" and a "premium" option in each category. In Chapter 6 we discussed the importance of also having an ultra high ticket item among your product mix.

These types of offerings can make up a very large percentage of your net profit even if you only sell a small number of units. It also attracts more affluent customers who shop based on prestige, service and convenience rather as opposed to low value customers who tend to be price shoppers. As mentioned in Chapter 6, a general rule of thumb is that about ten percent of your customers would pay you ten times more and one percent of your customers would pay you one hundred times more. Having only a single option leaves an enormous amount of money on the table.

Ultra high ticket items also help you benefit again from Cialdini's contrast principle. Your less affluent clients will see your standard products and services as being much more reasonably priced by comparison, while perhaps retaining many of the core features and benefits of the ultra high ticket item.

Lastly it will give clients an upgrade path. Something to aspire to. People always want what they can't have and having ultra high ticket items in your suite of products and services can keep alive their desire to buy from you in a future where they're in a better position to do so.

Frequency

Increasing the frequency with which your customers buy from you is another solid strategy for increasing lifetime value. There are many strategies for doing so but here are a few of my favorites.

Reminders. People live busy lives. They don't always remember to do things in a timely manner even when it's of benefit to them. Send reminders by post, email or SMS to remind them to do business with you again. The sending of regular reminders can be fully automated, so take advantage of technology to do some of the heavy lifting for you. Some worry about seeming too pushy. However, if you sell something of value, which benefits your customers, then you do them a great disservice by not selling to them regularly enough. Great candidates for reminder notices are products and services whose benefit or usefulness expires over time. Examples include car servicing, massages, ink cartridges, pet vaccinations and much more. What if you sell a product or service that has a longer lifespan, like for example real estate, cars or financial planning where you don't really know when the customer might be likely to buy? We covered this in Chapter 5. Keep in touch and continue building and developing a relationship through your nurturing system. It could be as simple as having a monthly postcard or newsletter. This keeps you top of mind so when they're ready to buy again you'll be top of mind.

Give them a reason to come back. My wife was recently shopping at a specialty shoe store which is almost an hour drive from our house. When she paid for her purchase she was given a voucher worth $30 for every hundred dollars she spent. She spent about $300 and ended up with a $90 voucher. The voucher was given to her at the checkout when she paid and had an expiry date that was about six months into the future. However, more importantly it only became valid from the day after its issue, so you couldn't just walk back in the store and use it immediately. You had to come back another day to use it. She came home and told me about all the amazing bargains she'd found out shopping as wives tend to do. Next she told me, "They had some shoes I think you'd like and I've got this voucher here for $60. It would be a shame to waste it." Guess where I was dragged the next day? With half my Saturday afternoon gone trying out shoes that I didn't know I needed we found ourselves at the register handing over another $200. The cashier told us the good news. We'd spent $200 so we were entitled to a $60 voucher. What happened next is a lesson in human psychology worth the additional $200. I watched my wife, who was tired of driving back and forth to this far flung shoe store, almost plead with the cashier not to give her the $60 voucher as she didn't want to drive all the way back and she also didn't want to "waste" the $60 voucher either. The cashier smiled and apologetically said it was store policy and that she had to give out the vouchers. With one simple tactic, the store had almost doubled the initial transaction value and created psychological pain associated with not coming in for repeat purchases. How could you use a similar tactic to encourage repeat business? Note this is completely different to discounting. This encouraged, almost forced future purchases.

Help them buy repeatedly with subscriptions. Some products or services like Internet access, insurance or electricity supply lend themselves naturally to a subscription business model. However, you need to think outside the square and take advantage of a revolution that's going on in the way that traditionally non-subscription products are being sold.

The Dollar Shave Club turned cheap disposable razor blades into a subscription service. How brilliant is that! Not only have they created enormous value and convenience for their customers but they now get to charge for their product every month until you say stop. Other product categories have followed suit enabling you to buy monthly subscriptions to cosmetics, underwear, fruit, socks, pet food and much more.

A big heavy bag of dog food now arrives automatically on my doorstep every six weeks. No more trekking to the pet store only to find it's out of stock. No more loading it in and out of the car and hauling it back home. It's automatic, I don't ever need to think about it again and my supplier is presumably thrilled with the predictable income stream. If you sell consumables of any type, couldn't you turn your product into a subscription service?

The side effect of this is that the customer's price-shopping radar generally turns off when buying products by subscription. Whereas previously I might have been tempted to look at discount offers on the particular brand of dog food I buy from the various pet food retailers in my area, now my dog food shopping radar is off. I know it's automatically taken care of every six weeks so why would I bother looking for it? Sure your customer might do a market check every so often but on a subscription service they don't need to make a purchasing decision every time. If you're delivering extra value in the way of convenience, your customers likely won't even care that you're charging them more. People understand that convenience has a price and for the most part they're ok with that.

Reactivation

If you're like most businesses you're sitting on a gold mine in the form of a list of past customers. Past customers have trusted you enough to cross the chasm between prospect and customer. They may have stopped buying from you for any number of reasons including a poor experience, better pricing elsewhere, moving out of the local area or simply apathy because you didn't give them a compelling reason to come back.

This list of past customers is of tremendous value because much of the hard work involved in getting prospects to know you, like and trust you has already been done. Now you just need to run a reactivation campaign to win them back. This is great for getting some quick wins and bringing in "fast cash."

Here are the basics of running a reactivation campaign:

1. Start by going through your customer database and pulling out names of past customers whom you haven't heard from or who haven't bought from you for a while. Obviously, you want to filter out any bad customers who you don't want back.

2. Create a strong offer to induce them back to you. A gift card, coupon or free offer with a strong call to action usually works well.

3. Contact these past customers and ask them why they haven't returned. If it's something you did wrong and if it's appropriate offer an apology and describe what corrective action you've taken. If they reactivate and start buying from you again, follow up with them afterwards to make them feel special.

Some great reactivation campaign themes and headlines are "We Miss You" or "Have We Done Something Wrong?" You can then describe to them how you've noticed they haven't bought from you in a while and you'd love to have them back and show them how special they are to you. You get the idea.

In an ideal world reactivation campaigns should be unnecessary but the reality is from time to time you'll mess up, lose out to a competitor or just get complacent with your marketing. A reactivation campaign can reboot the relationship and contribute significantly to increasing customer lifetime value.

Numbers Tell Us The Whole Story

I love a good story and storytelling is a big part of what we do as marketers. But when it comes to measuring and managing the success of your business, stories often obfuscate the truth.

If you've ever watched the television show *Shark Tank* you'll know exactly what I mean. In case you've never watched it, *Shark Tank* is a reality show where entrepreneurs pitch their business to a group of wealthy investors (referred to as sharks) in the hope of securing them as an investor. It always starts in the same predictable manner. The entrepreneur introduces their product or service, describes what problem it solves and usually demonstrates it. They usually end the presentation by telling the sharks what a great investment opportunity their business is. The sharks will then respond with a few softball questions and then inevitably comes the one that's on the mind of every prospective investor, "Tell us about your sales numbers." That's usually when most of the amateur entrepreneurs squirm and start telling a long convoluted story about why there are very few or no sales.

You also see great examples of these sort of weasel stories in many company prospectuses and investor reports. They dedicate pages upon pages telling their story. They brag about how great their products and service are, describe what great future prospects they have and back it all up with beautiful graphs illustrating a healthy growth trajectory. Then you get to their actual numbers and it's a sea of red. When I'm in the mood for some good fiction I skip the Stephen King novels and head for one of these reports instead. They can be a very entertaining read!

You've likely heard the often quoted management maxim, that **what gets measured gets managed**. Marketing is a game where you need to constantly measure, manage and improve your numbers. You don't need a long convoluted story. You just need the numbers because **numbers tell us the whole story**.

Your doctor just needs several key numbers and they pretty much know the state of your health. Your accountant just needs a few key numbers and they know the state of your business. The same is true of your marketing. You need to know and continually improve your numbers. In a moment I'll demonstrate to you why this is so powerful but for now here are some of the key numbers you need to know:

- **Leads.** This is the number of new leads that come to your business (lead capture and lead nurturing was covered in Chapters 4 and 5).
- **Conversion Rate.** This is the percentage of leads you converted into paying customers (we covered sales conversion in Chapter 6).
- **Average Transaction Value.** This is the average dollar amount that leads spend with you (we looked at several ways of increasing this number earlier in this chapter).
- **Break-even point.** This is the dollar amount you need to make to keep your doors open. It encompasses such things as rent, staff, utilities and any other ongoing operating expenses.

All of these numbers are typically measured on a monthly basis but depending on the size of your business you could measure them weekly or even daily. Now let's look at an example that demonstrates how powerful measuring, managing and improving these numbers is.

Imagine you run an online store that sells consumer electronics. You import the goods from China and have a healthy margin of 50% on each item listed in your online store. You get on average 8,000 visitors to your website each month and of these an average of 5% end up making a purchase. On average each customer spends $500 with you. Your break-even point which encompasses operating expenses such as running the warehouse, employing staff and hosting the website is $90,000 per month. So your monthly numbers look like this:

Leads	8,000
Conversion Rate	5%
Total Conversions:	400
Average Transaction Value	$500
Total Revenue:	$200,000
Gross Margin:	50%

Total Gross Profit:	$100,000
Break-even Point	$90,000
Total Net Profit:	$20,000

Now all we want to do is focus on improving three key numbers. We want to improve Leads, Conversion Rate and Average Transaction Value by just 10% each.

So you make your ad copy more compelling and instead of 8,000 visitors to your website, you get 8,800. Then you have an outrageous risk reversal guarantee which lifts your conversion rate from 5% to 5.5%. Lastly on your checkout page you have an upsell offer which lifts your average transaction value from $500 to $550. Your margin stays the same at 50% and fixed running expenses remain the same at $90,000 per month.

The numbers before and after your marketing optimizations look as follows:

	Before	**After**
Leads	8,000	8,800
Conversion Rate	5%	5.5%
Total Conversions:	400	484
Average Transaction Value	$500	$550
Total Revenue:	$200,000	$266,200
Gross Margin:	50%	50%
Total Gross Profit:	$100,000	$133,100
Break-even Point	$90,000	$90,000
Total Net Profit:	$10,000	$43,100

See what's happened? We've improved just three key numbers by only 10%, yet the result to the bottom line is a staggering 431% improvement. In the first scenario, the business owner was taking home $120,000 annually before taxes. In the second scenario, he takes home

$517,000 per year. Do you think that would have a massive impact to his life? Without a doubt it would.

Granted this is a very simplistic example and we're using cowboy math for the purposes of demonstration. However, it quickly becomes clear what a huge leverage point marketing is within a business.

Further optimizations could be made by increasing the gross margin through price increases or better buying power with the wholesale supplier. Perhaps some operating expenses could be cut through better automation and business systems.

The key point being that measuring, managing and improving your key marketing numbers even by an incremental amount can have massive impact on the end result. **Small hinges swing big doors**.

There are several other key metrics you need to measure and manage. As discussed in Chapter 3, Customer Acquisition Cost is an important metric that helps you figure out how much you spend on media spend on average to attract and convert a new customer. This in turns helps you figure out what kind of return on investment that particular media is giving you.

As discussed earlier in this chapter, your business should have a subscription or recurring element to it. If it doesn't yet, that's something you need to implement urgently. Here are some of the key metrics you need to measure and manage in a subscription or recurring business model:

- **Monthly Recurring Revenue**. Your total recurring billings. You want this number to be growing over time. If it's flattening out or declining you may have either a churn problem or a customer acquisition problem.
- **Churn Rate**. This is the percentage of recurring customers that cancel subscriptions or stop buying from you. Filling the bucket is great but not if it's leaking at a rapid rate.
- **Customer Lifetime Value**. The key metric that that this chapter is focused on. Increasing this number is where the money is.

Keeping a constant watch on your key numbers is one the best ways of managing your business and making sure that things are heading in the right direction. It avoids nasty surprises on quarterly or annual financial statements.

I highly recommend you keep track of these marketing metrics and any other significant numbers in your business on a company dashboard. A business dashboard can be as simple as whiteboard with the relevant numbers manually updated on a monthly or weekly basis or it can be more sophisticated like a real time screen or internal company web page. Commercial software solutions like Geckoboard can automatically pull data in realtime from a variety of sources. This makes measuring and managing your key metrics easy. Other metrics you may want to include on your dashboard could be Net Promoter Score if you measure it or number of customer complaints.

A business dashboard is a great early warning system for problems and can keep you and your team excited, motivated and accountable. Smart business owners also tie incentives to hitting key metrics. You might do something informal like taking the team out to dinner if the churn rate stays below a certain threshold or you might treat it more formally by tying performance reviews and bonuses to certain metrics.

Measuring, managing and improving your numbers daily, weekly or monthly is key to building a high growth business.

Polluted Revenue And The Unequal Dollar

Most entrepreneurs are driven and in the drive for growth and revenue sometimes not enough thought is given to the quality of that revenue. In this section I want to introduce you to the concept of the unequal dollar. It's absolutely key to helping you create a tribe of raving fans rather than transactional customers. This is absolutely key to your success. The difference between a customer who is just a transaction and one who is a raving fan is huge, even if the nominal dollar amount of the transaction is the same. This is because not all revenue is good and not all growth is good. For example, cancer grows but it's not the type of growth you want. Equally lethal to a business is growth of the wrong type of revenue.

Businesses need revenue like our bodies need air and water. Small businesses are often under resourced so it's forgivable that they're not too discriminating about where they take their revenue from. They're often in "eat what you kill" mode. If you drink polluted water or breathe polluted air you'll get sick. Similarly if you take on toxic customers you'll generate **polluted revenue**, which makes your businesses sick.

In other words, a dollar from suboptimal or toxic customers isn't equal to a dollar from a raving fan customer. This principle of the unequal dollar is vital to understand. Generally your customer base can be divided up into four categories[11]:

The Tribe. This is a set of customers that are raving fans, supporters and cheerleaders who promote your business and are actively conspiring for your success. This is healthy revenue that builds your business. Growing these types of customers is the key to being successful and achieving hyper-growth.

The Churners. Churners are customers who really can't afford you on the basis of either time or money. Because they can't afford you, you might have engage in overly aggressive sales and marketing tactics, overhyped promises or heavy discounts to get them to sign up. Then when they discover they're not a good fit, they churn out. They leave you and if you have too many of these, you catch a "churn flu," which can be fatal to your business. These types of customers can also create brand problems for your business as they often turn around and go back out into the marketplace and tell everybody that you're a liar or label you as dishonest.

The Vampires. Unlike churners, Vampires can afford you **but you can't afford them.** They consume a massively disproportionate amount of resources compared to your average customer while paying the same amount as other customers do. They usually aren't content to work with the teams that you have in place. They always need to talk to the CEO and they often terrorize and manipulate the CEO into terrorizing the team in their interest. They just suck the blood right out of your business.

---

[11]   A lot of the concepts in this section were devised by Richard Tripp, a specialist in hyper-growth and creator of the POV Method which helps categorise healthy versus unhealthy revenue.

The Snow Leopard. This might be your biggest customer, one who makes up a very large chunk of your revenue and pays you a lot of money. They're exquisite and beautiful but extremely rare and almost impossible to replicate. Most businesses have a client like this. They also tend to be customers who are fun to work with. They're so wonderful that the team and the leaders in the business love to spend a lot of time with them. Overall they're a bad investment because they're so rare and therefore don't represent a great growth strategy.

Another more formal way to categorize customers is using the Net Promoter Score (NPS). NPS has been created to measure customer loyalty and satisfaction. In NPS terminology customers are either promoters, detractors or passives. NPS can be as low as –100 (everybody is a detractor) or as high as +100 (everybody is a promoter). An NPS that is positive (i.e., higher than zero) is felt to be good, and an NPS of +50 is considered excellent. The Net Promoter Score is calculated based on responses to a single question,"How likely is it that you would recommend our company/product/service to a friend or colleague?" The score for this answer is most often based on a scale between one and ten. Those who respond with a score of 9 or 10 are labeled Promoters. Those who respond with a score of 0 to 6 are labeled Detractors. Those responding with 7 and 8 are labeled Passives. Often the scoring is then followed with an open-ended question asking for reason behind the customer's rating. These reasons can then be used by management for follow-up action.

Whether you use more formal metrics like NPS along with labels like Promoters and Detractors or you use less formal techniques and labels like Tribe, Churner and Vampire to categorize your customers, it's important that you don't treat all customers and revenue equally. Don't let yourself get fooled into thinking that all revenue is good.

Fire Problem Customers

Firing customers? That seems a very foreign concept to most business owners who are desperately trying to find new customers and new business. It may also seem bizarre that in a book all about marketing and customer acquisition that we have a section dedicated to firing customers. However, as discussed in the previous section, not all dollars are equal and not all revenue is good. You'll sometimes get to a stage where you know that you've got toxic customers and polluted revenue. You know it's sucking the life out of your business and you can't let it go on anymore.

Not firing problem customers is likely costing you huge amounts of time, money and aggravation. You've likely heard that old business cliché, "the customer is always right." I'm here to tell you the customer isn't always right. Rather the **right** customer is always right. Taking this cliché in its original form seriously will mean you live your business life as a doormat spending your time trying to please or retain problem customers like vampires and churners. Unlike red wine, problem clients don't get better with time.

First a clarification. I'm not talking about customers who have a legitimate cause for complaint. Customers who have a genuine complaint are valuable intelligence assets. It's often these sort of customers that can help you uncover weaknesses in your business. They may even reveal something that was causing you to lose business without you knowing because other unhappy customers didn't complain—they simply stopped buying from you. Fixing legitimate complaints from customers can strengthen your relationship with them and makes your business more robust. A customer who sees you responding to, and resolving their genuine complaint is far more likely to buy from you again and recommend you to others. They feel validated, respected and taken seriously.

Let's define problem customers. For whatever reason there's a percentage of the population who are never happy. They tend to fall into the categories of detractor/vampire/churner. They're always whining, dissatisfied and feeling like everyone's out to take advantage of them. You could shower them with gold and provide your product or service for free and they'll find something to complain about. These people are like a cancer sucking the life out of you and your business. I suggest you cut them loose as quickly as possible.

I have without exception, across multiple businesses and industries, found that it's the low value, price sensitive customers who complain the most, waste huge amounts of your time and who always need to be chased for payment. The high value customers who are the most profitable tend to pay on time, treat you with respect and value your services. It seems counterintuitive but it's been proved true in every business I've ever been involved with. I suggest that as part of your regular housekeeping activities, you fire these low value, problem clients.

As business owners we often get faked out by thinking as long as we keep the gross sales numbers high, there's bound to be enough net leftover to make it all worthwhile. However, if you ran a true profit and loss statement on these problem clients, which took into account all the time you spend chasing and appeasing them, you'd find very often that you make very little, if any, real profit on them. In fact most of them would likely result in a net loss when taking into account the low value they bring coupled with the time and energy needed to deal with them.

Another important reason you should fire low value customers is because apart from sucking up your financial resources, they are also causing you to lose out on opportunities. Firing problem customers frees up valuable time and resources which can be used for focusing on and building value with existing tribe members, as well as acquiring new ones. With the toxic customers taking up all your time and energy, it's often the high value, respectful customers who suffer a lack of attention. Don't give the squeaky wheels oil. Replace them.

Your tribe members are like the proverbial "good wife" taking care of things at home and keeping things running while the husband's out at strip clubs looking for love in all the wrong places. Your tribe are the ones that keep your lights on and stick with you and promote you despite you focusing on trying to appease vampires, trying to retain churners and throwing your time and resources at snow leopards.

Firing the detractors gives you the time needed to show more love to your high value tribe members. This builds loyalty and can very quickly result in an increase in lifetime value and healthy revenue that far outweighs the loss of the polluted revenue.

Another beneficial side effect of firing problem customers is that it creates scarcity without being disingenuous. It sends a message that you only have a limited supply and that you are very selective about who you'll work with. With limited supply, people have to play by your rules and pay accordingly.

Business should be fun. If you allow problem customers to suck the fun out of it, then you're losing out on one of the major benefits of running your own business. If it's no longer fun, no amount of money can compensate for being miserable. If it's no longer fun you're likely not doing it right. Take time out periodically to review which customers are causing you the most pain in your business. Then channel Donald Trump and deliver them the news they deserve. You'll feel like a huge weight has been taken off your shoulders and you'll have renewed energy to focus on high value tribe members.

Better still you can kill two birds with one stone by sending your problem customers to your direct competitors. You'll be freeing yourself of them while lumping your competitors with them.

Chapter 8 Action Item:
How Will You Increase Customer Lifetime Value?
Fill in square #8 of your 1-Page Marketing Plan

Chapter 9

Orchestrating And Stimulating Referrals

Chapter 9 Summary

Orchestrating and stimulating referrals is an active process. Many businesses wish and hope for referrals but don't have a deliberate system for making them happen. By implementing some simple tactics you can make the flow of referrals a more reliable part of your marketing process.

Highlights covered in this chapter include:

- Why relying on word of mouth is a losing strategy.
- How to ask for referrals without looking needy or desperate.
- The "Law of 250" and how it relates to getting an ongoing stream of referral business.
- The psychology behind referral marketing and how to compel existing customers to want to give you referrals.
- How to create a winwin scenario with joint ventures.
- How to profit by referring your customers to others.
- What "branding" really is and how to build brand equity in your business.

Don't Rely On A Free Lunch

Whenever I speak to business owners about how they market themselves, "word of mouth" almost always comes up as the primary or only form of marketing they rely on. This used to shock me but now I've come to expect it. When I talk about "word of mouth" marketing here I'm talking about the passive type where you hope that by doing a good job that the word will spread and more customers will come your way.

Notice that the name of this chapter isn't sit and wait for referrals? It's called **orchestrating** and **stimulating** referrals. This implies something very active on your part to make referrals happen. Yet many business owners see referrals as something that's out of their hands and is something that just (hopefully) happens. Whilst passive word-of-mouth marketing is great, it's an extremely slow and unreliable way of building a business. Assuming you do everything right, it can take many years, even decades, to build a successful business on the back of word of mouth alone. As discussed in Chapter 2 having only a single source of new business is extremely dangerous but being unable to control that source makes it doubly so.

Word of mouth is the business equivalent of a free lunch. Sure it's nice when it comes your way and you appreciate it, but do you really want to rely on it to feed yourself and your family? By being solely reliant on word of mouth, you're putting the fate of your business in the hands of others—hoping they both like you and remember you often enough to regularly send new business your way. This is an extremely dangerous path to be on. If it's similar to what you do in your business, now's the time to start building a much more robust referral marketing system. You need to actively orchestrate and stimulate referrals, rather than just hope and wait for them to happen.

The key part of the problem seems to be that business owners don't want to seem needy or desperate in actively asking for referrals. They feel like asking for referrals is like begging or asking for a favor and that's certainly not the kind of positioning I'd want you to adopt.

It's important to understand the psychology behind referral marketing before we get onto specific tactics. Think back to the last time you recommended a restaurant or a movie to a friend. Were you doing so as a favor to the restaurant owner or movie theatre chain? Unlikely. In all likelihood you wanted your friend to have a great experience. You made the referral because it made **you** look and feel good. That's the exact same concept we want to use in our referral marketing, but rather than waiting and hoping someone discovers us and shares, we want to orchestrate and stimulate the process. We want to make it more deliberate and reliable.

Ask And You Shall Receive

Remember the world's greatest salesman, Joe Girard, whom we introduced in Chapter 5? Part of the reason he started sending greeting cards to his list of clients monthly was because of the "Law of 250." After attending a Catholic funeral, Joe looked into the visitor book and counted the numbers of people who signed it at each funeral. He noticed that on average it was about 250 people. Later he sold a car to man who ran a funeral home and after the sale asked him how many people on average attended the funerals he conducts. The man replied "About 250." Another time Joe and his wife were attending a wedding and he asked the owner of the catering business what the average number of guests at a wedding were. "About 250 from the bride's side, and another 250 from the groom's," came the answer. That's when Joe came to the realization that most people have about 250 people in their lives who are important enough to invite to a wedding or to a funeral.

From that he figured that every person he did business with represented 250 potential referrals, if he did a great job or 250 enemies if he did a crappy job. So he set about building relationships rather than thinking transactionally and just selling cars. One of the things he did was follow up with new customers and ask how their new car was going. If it was going well, he'd ask for a referral. If it wasn't, he'd fix the problem and then ask for a referral.

This brings us to **one of the best strategies for getting what you want in business and indeed in life—just ask.**

So many people just wait to be discovered, wait to be picked, wait to be referred to. You, however, are an entrepreneur which means **you**

196

make things happen for yourself. You don't just wait for them to happen to you. With this in mind one of the best ways to get referrals is by straight out asking for them from customers for whom you've delivered a good result. It's amazing how many business owners hope for referrals yet rarely ask for them. Something as simple as:

> *"Mr. Customer, it's been such a pleasure working with you. If you know anyone who's in a similar situation as yourself we'd love you to give them one of these gift cards which entitles them to $100 off their first consultation with us. One of the reasons we're able to keep the cost of our service down is because we get a lot of our business through referrals from people like you."*

See what's going on here:

- We're acknowledging them and appealing to their ego. People love being acknowledged.
- We're not asking them for a favor but instead offering something valuable they can give to someone in their network.
- We're giving them a reason why they should give us referrals—a reason that had directly benefited them.

By putting a system around generating referrals, we've dramatically increased the reliability of word of mouth marketing. And while not everyone will give you referrals, many will and it sure beats just passively hoping.

One of the things you can be almost sure of is that your customers know other people who are similar to themselves. It's human nature to be attracted to people with the same likes, interests and situations as us.

Another excellent strategy is to make known during your sales or customer onboarding process that you **expect** them to give you referrals as a natural course of doing business with you.

> *"Mr. Customer, I'm going to do an awesome job for you, but I do need your help also. Most of our new business comes through referrals. This means that rather than paying for advertising to get new clients, we*

can just pass the cost savings directly to you. We typically get about three referrals from each new customer. When we're finished working together and you're 100% satisfied with the work we've done, I'd really appreciate it if you could keep in mind three or more other people that we could also help."

Again breaking it down we are:

- Letting them know that they're going to get a great result
- Showing them a direct benefit that they're going to be, or already are, deriving by referring to us
- Creating an expectation of a certain number referrals (without being too pushy) so that they can start thinking ahead of time about who would be suitable
- Leaving the power with them by telling them that it's subject to us doing a great job for them

Relying on the goodwill of others is not my idea of being an entrepreneur. By increasing the reliability of word of mouth marketing, you take back control of your lead flow and build a solid foundation for rapid business growth.

Who Has Your Clients Before You?

As business owners we sometimes don't see ourselves within the bigger picture of our customer's buying behavior. We just see their interaction with us and market ourselves to acquire more and more customer interactions.

There's nothing wrong with that of course. But when we start to look at the bigger picture, we can start to uncover profits that were previously hidden. It's like finding a $50 bill in a jacket you haven't worn in a while but on a much bigger and more profitable scale!

Your customer's transaction with you is one of many they will make that day.

Before their transaction with you they did business with someone else and after you they'll do business with someone else.

The transactions may or may not be related but one thing is for certain—someone had your customers before you did and in all likelihood they spent a good deal of money on sales and marketing to acquire that customer.

Finding other complimentary businesses that your customer deals with before they deal with you can help you uncover untapped profits in your business. Setting up a joint venture (JV) arrangement with one or more of these businesses that is not in direct competition with you can be a cheap or free source of leads.

If you're a lawyer, an accountant might make a great source of new leads. If you're a car detailer, a mechanic could be your source of leads. If you're a pet food retailer, a vet might be your ideal source of new customers.

While this may seem obvious, it's rarely done and it is even more rarely done well.

Setting up a JV arrangement can be tricky. The most obvious and direct route is to pay either a finder's fee or a commission for incoming leads or sales.

However, some business owners may not feel comfortable about taking cash for leads they send you and in some industries this may not even be legal. While it's smart to pay for leads of known buyers who are "hot," there are other less direct ways that work just as well or better.

One awesome strategy involves creating a gift card or voucher for your products or services. Let's say for example your business is "Mike's Pet World"—a pet food retailer. You could create an arrangement with a local vet. Find out what kind of pet food this vet recommends to his clients, then create a voucher or gift card that he can give away to new clients.

The beauty of this is that it is goodwill all round, no sales pressure, no conflicts of interest. The vet would say something like, "I recommend XYZ dog food. You can buy it at most pet food retailers but you're a good customer so here's a $50 voucher which you can redeem at Mike's Pet World who are down the road. They always carry plenty of stock of XYZ dog food."

It's a win-win for every party involved. The vet creates massive good-will with the customer because he is essentially handing them $50 for free. The customer receives an unexpected discount. You, as the owner of Mike's Pet World, acquire a new customer whose lifetime value is potentially huge in exchange for a voucher with a face value of $50 (and a wholesale cost which is much less). You also get transferred much of the goodwill the customer already has with their vet.

Now it's true not all customers will redeem a gift card or voucher but the vast majority will. It feels too much like throwing out money to throw out a voucher or gift card that you know has a monetary value associated with it. Let's say that you conservatively calculate that the average lifetime value of a new customer at your pet store is $5,000.

You've given away a part of the profit from a sale you would have never have had. Genius!

Flipping it back the other way, you should look to see who has or wants your clients after you're done servicing them. This can become a great secondary source of revenue to you, while increasing the value of your offering to the end customer. Here are a few ways to monetize your existing customer base in this way:

- **Sell the leads.** There's very likely someone else in a complementary but noncompetitive line of business that would be willing to pay handsomely for hot, qualified leads. One caveat here is to ensure that you have your customer's explicit permission to pass on their details.

- **Exchange the leads.** If you didn't want to, or it's not appropri-ate, to accept payment for leads you could set up a two-way lead exchange program with someone else in a complementary busi-ness. They send you their customers and you send them yours. Again the same caveat as selling leads applies. Never give out your customer's confidential details without their permission.

- **Resell complementary products and services.** You could buy complementary products and services on a wholesale or white label basis and resell these to your customer base. The benefit of this model is that you maintain full control of the relationship and never hand over your customer details to a third party.

- **Become an affiliate referral partner.** This is similar to the model of selling leads except that instead of being paid per lead, you get paid a commission on sales made by the third party you're referring to. This can be extremely profitable especially in scenarios where you get a trailing commission on all future sales. Refer once and get paid forever (or at least a long time). Many people in industries such as insurance, telecommunications and finance have built highly profitable businesses based on this model.

Look at who has your customers before you and after you and find ways of creating value in both directions. This can become an important source of new customers and new revenue for your business.

Building Your Brand

There's an enormous amount of confusion, especially among small businesses, as to what a brand is. A search on the Internet gives the following diverse range of answers:

"It is the emotional and psychological relationship you have with your customers."

"A type of product manufactured by a particular company under a particular name."

"The name, term, design, symbol, or any other feature that identifies one seller's product distinct from those of other sellers."

"It is the idea or image of a specific product or service that consumers connect with, by identifying the name, logo, slogan, or design of the company who owns the idea or image."

All of these are only partial answers. I like to eliminate fluff and keep things simple. So here is my definition: a brand is the personality of a business. In fact you can use the well-understood word "personality" as a direct substitute for "brand." That instantly clarifies the meaning.

Think of your business as a person. What attributes make up its personality?

- What's its name?
- What does it wear? (i.e. design)
- How does it communicate? (i.e. positioning)
- What are its core values and what does it stand for? (i.e. brand promise)
- Who does it associate with? (i.e. target market)
- Is it well-known? (i.e. brand awareness)

This personality varies dramatically between businesses. Toyota and Rolls Royce both produce functionally the same product, but their answers to the above are very different.

Some small businesses look at the flashy advertising campaigns of well-known brands like Apple, Coca-Cola etc. and get caught up thinking that they also need to spend time, money and effort building "brand awareness." That's putting the cart before the horse. Let me ask you a simple question: What came first, the sales or the brand awareness? The sales of course. It's true that as a company gets bigger, brand awareness does feed sales. However, don't look at what they do now as big companies. Look at what these businesses did to get big in the first place.

When they were small, they certainly didn't spend huge amounts of money on flashy ads and brand awareness. They hustled, they closed deals and sold their products. If Apple and Coca-Cola didn't concentrate on sales to begin with, they wouldn't exist today and there'd certainly be no awareness of them.

That's why I tell small business owners the best form of brand building is selling. If a brand is the personality of a business, what better way is there for someone to understand that personality than by buying from you.

As we discussed in the starting chapter, trying to emulate the marketing practices of large businesses is a major mistake.

When all is said and done, branding is something you do **after** someone has bought from you, rather than something you do to induce them to buy from you. In the same way that you get a sense of someone's personality after you've dealt with them, so too it is with your business and its personality or brand.

Brand equity is the goodwill you build up that compels people to do business with you rather than your competitor. I once heard brand equity described as customers crossing the road to buy from you even though there's a supplier of an equivalent product on their side of the road.

The things in your business that cause customers to figuratively or literally "cross the road" to buy from you, is your brand equity. This can manifest itself in the form of customer loyalty, repeat business or even a price premium you can charge for your product or service. Importantly, it's also the key to stimulating the virtuous cycle of referrals.

For me, nothing illustrates this better than seeing queues of people lining up for the latest Apple gadget while their competitors with plentiful stock and no queues get much lower demand. This kind of brand equity is born out of amazing previous customer experiences, which turn customers into raving fans. This is something that simply can't be bought with hype-filled "brand awareness" campaigns. No one at Apple has to ask you to "tell your friends," you just do because the incredible brand equity they've built up.

As a small business your best hope for emulating this is focusing on sales and then turning your customer into a tribe of raving fans. This is the advice I give to any small-to-medium business wanting to work on branding.

Chapter 9 Action Item:
How Will You Orchestrate And Stimulate Referrals?
Fill in square #9 of your 1-Page Marketing Plan

Conclusion

A Bird's Eye View Of What We've Covered

We've covered a lot of ground in our journey through the nine squares that make up The 1-Page Marketing Plan. It's useful at this stage to take a step back and look at a high level, visual overview of the direct response marketing lifecycle.

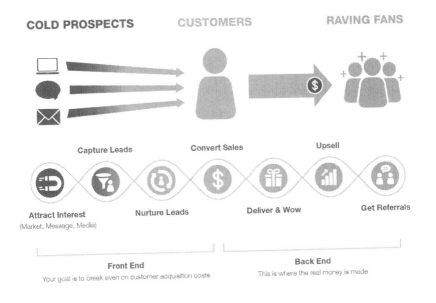

> ## To download your copy of the Direct Response Marketing Lifecycle visit 1pmp.com

This along with your personal implementation of the 1-Page Marketing Plan will give you a solid foundation for marketing success in your business.

As mentioned in the preface of this book, very few if any of the ideas in this book are my original inventions. They are mostly proven strategies, tactics and concepts taken from decades of testing and measuring by the direct response marketing masters. However, The 1-Page Marketing Plan is an **implementation** breakthrough. It's designed to dramatically simplify the understanding of direct response marketing and speed up its implementation in your business. Remember it's all about implementation. I'll reiterate—**knowing and not doing is the same as not knowing**. You need to make the mistakes, risk looking foolish and invest in yourself and your business. In my experience I've found that entrepreneurs fail to implement for one of the following three reasons:

1. **Paralysis By Analysis:** They keep trying to learn more or get stuck chasing the latest bright shiny object in the hope that they'll get everything perfect the first time around. You'll never get everything perfect the first time. You only truly learn by doing. Don't let perfectionism become a source of procrastination to you. Remember **80% out the door is better than 100% in the drawer**. Successful entrepreneurs have a bias for action, implement quickly and course correct along the way. As one of my early mentors Mal Emery would say, "money loves speed." The best time to plant a tree is yesterday. The second best time to plant a tree is today. If you've been putting off building and implementing a marketing system for your business then it's time to plant that tree and get started immediately so that you can reap the fruits of your labor in the future.

2. **Inability To Delegate:** As mentioned in Chapter 5, business is a team sport. I don't know of any successful entrepreneur who doesn't have a team behind them. You have only twenty-four hours a day, so the only way you can get more achieved in a day is by using other people's time. Even more importantly than other people's time is other people's specialist expertise. This can reduce your learning by trial and error by years. What you don't know **will** hurt you. Hiring specialist expertise will save you time, money and huge amounts of frustration. The ability to get independent and sometimes difficult people to

all go in one direction working on behalf of your cause is skill you should commit to mastering. This is what the late great Jim Rohn referred to as "herding cats" and almost nothing pays more than mastering this skill.

3. **"My Business Is Different"**: Pretty much any conceivable problem you have or are going to encounter has been solved by someone at some time. Many of the solutions to your marketing problems are in this book. Some business owners mistakenly think "my business is different, this won't work for me" or "my customers are different, they'd never respond to something like that." The strategies and tactics in this book are time tested and proven over many decades. They've worked in almost every category and type of business you could care to imagine from trades to consulting to medical service and much, much more. The reason the same stuff works over time and across different business types is that you're dealing with humans—big bags of emotion. This doesn't change over time or across industry. People behave in a remarkably predictable manner, which is why I know that these direct response marketing principles **will** work for your business. There's no leverage in trying to figure out why these things won't work for you. Your effort is far better spent trying to figure out how to make it work for you.

Time Is Not Money

As entrepreneurs, we only get paid for bringing value to the market—not for time. Sure it takes time to deliver value but we only get paid for the value. If we deliver a huge amount of value to the marketplace, we get a huge payday. If we flop, we make a loss. That's a risk most people aren't willing to take. Most people want to get paid for time—work an hour, get paid for an hour. They want to avoid loss at all costs. Making gain to them is a nice-to-have but their real objective is pain avoidance. There's nothing wrong with that but the mindsets are worlds apart. Put simply entrepreneurs work in the results economy whereas most other people work in the time and effort economy.

The money we make as entrepreneurs is an automatic side effect of creating value. If our focus is on bringing value to the market, it will stop us from making all kinds of foolish mistakes. We'll treat customers with the long-term in mind rather than being transactional or trying to make a quick buck. The products we create or the services we deliver won't be half-baked. Focusing on the cause (value) rather than the effect (making money) will lead to much greater long-term success.

Most of this book has been focused on getting, retaining and satisfying customers through effective marketing. These are the tasks that create the most value in your business and facilitate rapid growth. Almost everything else is overhead.

The more times we create value by getting, retaining and satisfying a customer, the more we get paid. Unfortunately many business owners get distracted "playing business." Playing business is when you do peripheral activities that don't really create much value. Some examples of "playing business" include things like constantly checking email and endless, nonsense meetings that have no real point or agenda.

Instead of playing business, you must **do** business. Winning in business requires you to have a relentless focus on the activities that deliver value. You must fight a daily battle with distraction, interruption and procrastination. If you allow yourself to be distracted from the value creating work of getting, retaining and satisfying customers your business will struggle or fail. There are always things to do that are more fun or seemingly urgent.

We rationalize playing business but in reality there are really only a few value building activities which you need to do daily—marketing being key among them. It's important to understand that marketing isn't an event, it's a process. It's something you do daily to build massive value in your business and deliver massive value to your customers.

Your view of time affects everything you do in your business. For the entrepreneur time is **not** money. Value is money. Time is just one of the inputs it takes to deliver value to the market. Make marketing a daily process. Create your own 1-Page Marketing Plan and most importantly **implement** the plan. Spend time daily **doing** business and building value.

Lipstick On A Pig

An enormous amount of your success is dependent on the vehicle you choose. Some businesses are a Ferrari and adding marketing just exponentially skyrockets their success. Whereas other businesses are a beat-up old jalopy and adding marketing is like putting lipstick on a pig.

In a time when new technology is disrupting industries that have been around for decades or centuries, it's valuable to continually evaluate whether your business or industry is in the sunrise or sunset phase. Good times don't last forever. Just ask brick and mortar bookstores, record stores and traditional news media giants.

Around the year 1900 there were 100,000 horses in New York. London in 1900 had 11,000 cabs, all horse-powered. There were also several thousand buses, each of which required 12 horses per day, for a total of more than 50,000 horses. In addition, there were countless carts, drays, and wains, all working constantly to deliver the goods needed by the rapidly growing population of these cities. All transport, whether of goods or people, was drawn by horses.

If you had a horse-related business, then business was booming. Everything from clearing away the huge amounts of horse manure to grooming, feeding and housing the ever-growing population of horses.

Fast forward a few short years to the advent of electrification and the development of the internal-combustion engine that brought new ways to move people and goods around. By 1912, cars in New York outnumbered horses, and in 1917 the city's last horse-drawn streetcar made its final run.

So in twelve years your business went from being on top of the world to losing more than half its revenue. Five years after that you were bust and all your knowledge, industry connections and skills were totally obsolete. Failing to anticipate how changes in technology will affect your business or industry and taking action accordingly can be fatal to your business.

Kodak invented digital photography, yet despite this they could not or did not use this early lead to its advantage. It let other competitors eat its lunch. Borders finally got into e-books but it was too little, too late and consequently it also paid the ultimate price.

209

When the guy running his booming horse business in the early 1900s started to see these new fangled electric streetcars appearing, he might have chuckled to himself and thought that this form of transport was just a passing fad. After all, horses had been used as means of transport for thousands of years.

Then a few years on, when more and more of his revenue was being eroded by the new technology, he might have started pining for the "good old days" when things were going well. He might have even become angry about what was happening and expected the government to intervene. See anything similar happening today?

Various industries including manufacturing, news media and brick and mortar retail are either in crisis or on the verge of crisis. Globalization, the Internet and new technology is hurting them—big time. They are whining and crying about the state of things, lobbying for government intervention and hoping the good old days will soon return. But the good old days aren't coming back—at least not for them.

Why don't they just embrace the new technology and get onboard with it? Some of them will but most won't. The reason most won't is because they have the same mindset as a turkey does.

Nassim Taleb, best-selling author of *The Black Swan*, tells the story of a turkey who is fed by a farmer every morning for 1,000 days. Eventually the turkey comes to expect that every visit from the farmer means more good food. That's all that has ever happened, so the turkey figures that's all that can and will ever happen. In fact, on day 1,000 it's at the peak of its confidence. After all it now has 1,000 day's worth of track record on which to base its confidence. With a track record like that what can possibly go wrong? But then day 1,001 arrives. It's two days before Thanksgiving and when the farmer shows up this time he hasn't got food in his hand, instead he has a recently sharpened axe. The turkey learns very quickly that its expectations were catastrophically off the mark—that the good old days weren't going to last forever. So now Mr. Turkey is dead.

Don't be a turkey and don't run your business like one. In times past almost all the value of a business was in its physical assets. Things like real estate, plant and equipment, inventory and distribution infrastructure.

Today almost all the value of a business is in the eyeballs it has access to and the customer base it has acquired.

Look at what's happening today and the central role that acquiring customers through effective marketing plays:

- Uber, the world's largest taxi company owns no vehicles.
- Facebook, the world's most popular media owner creates no content.
- Alibaba, the most valuable retailer owns no inventory.
- Airbnb, the world's largest accommodation provider owns no real estate.

Just these four businesses are worth hundreds of billions of dollars.

Your ultimate competitive advantage is in anticipating change and taking action accordingly. It's going to take guts, you'll have to take risks and you'll have to invest in research and new technology. You need to constantly be pondering questions such as:

- What business do I need to be in?
- What technologies are coming that are going to disrupt my industry?
- How can I take advantage of the coming changes in technology rather than fight them?

You need constant strategic innovation—innovation that your customer cares about.

Skunkworks projects are one of the best ways to stay abreast of emerging technology while still continuing to run your current operation. A famous example of a skunkworks project is the first Apple Macintosh computer. Google has even made it part of their company's culture by allocating 20% of employee time on side projects that interest them. Hugely successful Google products such as Gmail, Adsense and Google News have come from these skunkworks projects.

What resources are you investing in emerging technologies and trends in your industry?

Day 1,001 is coming for your business and your industry and if you aren't ready with a new plan, your business could well suffer the fate of the turkey.

Having a culture of innovation, anticipating what's coming in your industry and running some skunkworks projects in your business will give your business a massive competitive advantage.

Your Transition From Business Owner To Marketer

Einstein's famous definition of insanity, "doing the same thing over and over again and expecting different results," is well-known but rarely acted upon.

At the start of every new year people make "resolutions." Typical ones are to lose weight, quit smoking and get out of debt. They hope that things will magically become better for them as the clock strikes midnight on the 31st of December. When they hit week two or three of the new year, their resolutions become a distant memory as they return to routine, old habits and the daily grind.

Resolutions are a close cousin of wishes—basically nothing more than goals which have no plan or action behind them. Chances are if nothing changes in your regular routine, nothing will change in your business or personal life.

One of the commonalities amongst high growth businesses is that they have a strong focus on marketing. They make marketing a regular routine in their business and execute their marketing plan continuously.

Conversely, failed and struggling businesses either neglect marketing altogether or do random acts of marketing with no plan or structure. They try random tactics once or twice and give up when they don't see immediate success. That's not a marketing plan—that's a recipe for disaster.

Others mistakenly believe that having a great product or service is enough to "get the word out there." The graveyards of failed businesses are full of businesses that had excellent products and services. For the most part they failed because those running them didn't pay enough attention to marketing. Remember, **no one knows how good**

your products or services are until after the sale. Before they buy, they only know how good your marketing is. Put simply **the best marketer wins every time**.

If you're serious about business success then now's the time to take decisive action. It's time to decide to become a great marketer and transform yourself from a business owner to a marketer who owns a business. Once you make this exciting transformation you and your business will never be the same again.

It's my belief that this book is a marketing implementation breakthrough in that it makes creating and implementing your own marketing plan easy. It can help you start or accelerate your journey from business owner to a marketer.

Marketing is the master skill of business. It will help you make your current business a success and importantly it will help make other businesses and enterprises you may be involved with in the future successful.

Throughout this book, you've been the recipient of some extremely valuable information. It's information that most of your competitors will never know or seek out. That puts you at a huge advantage—if you take action. I urge you to take action. As mentioned at the beginning of this book **knowing and not doing is the same as not knowing**. If you continue to do what you've always done, you'll continue to get the same results you've always gotten.

Building a successful business enables you to live life on your own terms. You deserve business success and it is attainable for YOU. I invite you on that journey of building an extraordinary business and living life on your own terms.

About The Author

Allan Dib is a serial entrepreneur, rebellious marketer and technology expert.

He has started and grown multiple businesses in various industries including IT, telecommunications and marketing.

One of his previous businesses was in the telecommunications industry where he faced heated competition from multi-billion dollar, multinational competitors. Allan grew this business from startup to four years later being named by Business Review Weekly (BRW) as one of Australia's fastest growing companies—earning a spot on the coveted BRW Fast 100 list.

Allan is passionate about helping businesses find new and innovative ways to leverage technology and marketing to facilitate rapid business growth.

As a highly sought after business coach, consultant and public speaker, he frequently shares his proven strategies and cutting edge tactics with people all over the world.

Allan can be contacted directly via email at allan@successwise.com

Information about his books, courses and other training materials can be found at successwise.com